Kid Safe

Also by Susan K. Golant:

How to Have a Smarter Baby
   with Dr. Susan Ludington-Hoe

No More Hysterectomies
   with Vicki Hufnagel, M.D.

Disciplining Your Preschooler and Feeling Good About It
   with Mitch Golant, Ph.D.

Kindergarten: It Isn't What It Used to Be
   with Mitch Golant, Ph.D.

The Joys and Challenges of Raising a Gifted Child

Getting Through to Your Kids
   with Mitch Golant, Ph.D.

Finding Time for Fathering
   with Mitch Golant, Ph.D.

Hardball for Women
   with Pat Heim, Ph.D.

Kid Safe

A Parent's Guide to Keeping Your Child Safe

by

Susan K. Golant

Galahad Books • New York

Previously published as FIFTY WAYS TO KEEP YOUR CHILD SAFE
Copyright © 1992 by RGA Publishing Group, Inc., and Susan K. Golant.

First Galahad Books edition published in 1995.

Galahad Books
A division of Budget Book Service, Inc.
386 Park Avenue South
New York, NY 10016

Galahad Books is a registered trademark of Budget Book Service, Inc.

Published by arrangement with Lowell House, a division of
RGA Publishing Group, Inc.

Library of Congress Catalog Card Number: 95-075032

ISBN: 0-88365-890-9

Printed in the United States of America.

To Cherie and Aimee

Contents

Part III. In the World

Part IV. Health Watch

Acknowledgments

I would like to express my gratitude to the American Heart Association, the American Lung Association, the American Red Cross, Child Care Action Campaign, Childhelp USA, the Los Angeles Police Department, the Los Angeles Fire Department, the Los Angeles County Regional Drug and Poison Control Center, the Lead Institute, the National Center for Missing and Exploited Children, the National AIDS Information Clearing House, the National Safe Kids Campaign, the National Safety Council, Project D.A.R.E. (Drug Abuse Resistance Education), the U.S. Department of Justice, and the UCLA School of Public Health for sharing their consumer materials with me. I am also grateful to Charlene Solomon, Linda Marsa, Dr. Pat Heim, and Allen Drapkin, D.D.S., for going out of their way to assist me in this project.

And, as always, I feel indebted to my husband, Mitch, for his ever present support and love, and our two wonderful daughters, who probably taught me more about safety than I ever really wanted to know.

Introduction

Kid Safe

According to Dr. C. Everett Koop, former United States Surgeon General and chairman of the National Safe Kids Campaign, "If a disease were killing our children in the proportions that accidents are, people would be outraged and demand that this killer be stopped." The truth is, accidents are the leading cause of childhood fatalities today.

But despite their prevalence, accidents aren't our only worries. These days, we must also pay attention to how our kids fare on the streets. Do they know about the dangers of smoking, alcohol, and drug abuse? Do they understand how AIDS is transmitted? Do they know how to eat properly? Can they protect themselves from people who would exploit their bodies? Can they keep themselves safe when we're at work? After all, the one eventuality parents fear most is that their children won't make it to adulthood safe and sound.

I know. I'm the mother of two college-age daughters. Above and beyond all else, I've understood my role as parent to mean that I should nurture and protect my children physically, emotionally, medically, and environmentally. It hasn't been easy. Indeed, this seems the perfect book for an overprotective semiparanoid parent like me to write! Kids, after all, have minds of their own, and society presents them with many opportunities to get into hot water. And I've probably agonized over each and every one of those opportunities.

But regardless of the potential hazards inherent in growing up today, the threat of your child's endangerment need not immobilize you. Tragedies can be avoided if you follow a few commonsense safety guidelines.

This book will help you do just that. It will answer your many questions on how to keep your three- to twelve-year-old child safe. In these pages, you'll learn:

- How to test your dishes for lead
- Where to store and how to deal with poisons
- What your child should know about bicycle, skate, and skateboard safety
- What to do about radon gas and asbestos
- How your child can remain safe from sexual abuse and kidnapping
- How to prepare for earthquakes and other natural disasters
- How to prevent the spread of sexually transmitted diseases
- What constitutes and how to practice good nutrition
- What makes a good day-care center
- How best to prevent substance abuse
- Where to place smoke alarms

The information in *Kid Safe* is divided into six sections for your easy reference: At Home, On the Road, In the World, Health Watch, Substance Abuse Prevention, and Fire Awareness. Each section provides myriad tips on specific topics. You can read the book cover to cover, or you can refer to each section as the need arises. In some instances, the advice may repeat, as in the case of garage safety and poisons or fire protection. This was done intentionally: The material is so important that it applies to several areas. What's more, reference is faster and more convenient this way: If you're in the midst of a hazardous situation, you'll want to be able to quickly refer to the section most applicable to your immediate needs.

In addition, although this book deals primarily with prevention, I've included some information on first aid: Taking the proper measures when an injury occurs can prevent more serious complications and keep harm at a minimum.

Rest assured that these commonsense tips come from firsthand parenting experience as well as from such authorities as the National Safety Council, the National Safe Kids Campaign, the Lead

Institute, the American Heart Association, the American Lung Association, the American Red Cross, the American Dental Association, and the Department of Health and Human Services, to name a few.

It is my privilege to compile and share this information with you in the hope that it helps your youngsters grow into healthy and productive adults.

PART
I

At
Home

Know How to Deal with Poisons

A poison is any substance—solid, liquid, or gas—that can cause injury or death if misused. Some substances, such as nonaspirin painkiller or mouthwash, can be relatively harmless in small doses yet lethal if a child swallows too much of them. Poisons can be inhaled (cleaning fluids, fertilizer sprays, carbon monoxide), swallowed (drugs, mothballs, drain cleaner), absorbed through the skin (insecticides, poison ivy), or injected (bee stings, intravenous drugs, snake bites).

According to the National Safety Council, almost 5,000 people die each year from accidental poisonings. Of the 1.3 million nonfatal poisonings that occur annually, almost two thirds—800,000—involve children. And most of these accidents could have been avoided. Here's how you can protect your child from being hurt by toxic substances.

Medications

Make sure to choose over-the-counter products packaged in childproof containers. Ask your pharmacist for prescriptions in childproof containers. Never leave medications out where they may be within your youngster's reach, on your night table, for instance. Such flavored or chocolated products as Pepto Bismol and Ex-Lax are not candy and should also be kept out of reach in the medicine cabinet. If you carry these products in your purse, your child may mistake them for treats.

Never allow a young child to administer her medication herself.

You should give it to her in the proper amount, and leave the medication with the school nurse to give during the school day. Be careful not to take medications in front of your child, who may imitate you later. And never refer to medicine as "candy."

For more safety precautions you can take around the medicine cabinet, see 14, Practice Safety in the Bathroom.

Household Products

Be careful to store cleaning products, insecticides, and other toxic substances in cabinets well out of reach of children. Make sure the cabinet is secured with a childproof or combination lock. (By all means, avoid letting your kids learn to open these cabinets by watching you!) Keep a constant eye on your youngsters while you're using potentially toxic household products. Kids have been known to take a sip when a parent's back is turned. My children were raised to keep away from anything I called "poison."

Read the labels of household products. These usually provide antidotes and instructions in case of poisoning. They also give instructions for proper use, such as only in a well-ventilated area. Never mix ammonia and bleach; the two combined can create a poisonous gas. Furthermore, never put poisonous products in unlabeled containers that you've used in the past for food. It's easy to forget and confuse the two. You'll find much more on household cleaning products in 2, Store and Use Cleaning Supplies Safely.

Poisonous Plants

More than 100 house and garden plants are poisonous. (See the Resource Guide to find out how to obtain a list of these.) Keep such highly poisonous plants as azalea and oleander out of your home and away from your property. Teach your children to recognize these plants as well as poison ivy, oak, and sumac (which have leaves that grow in clusters of three). It's wise to learn the scientific names of plants in your home in case you need to identify them for poison control or for your child's doctor. Ask the horticulturist at your local plant nursery for advice, and label your house plants with both their common and scientific names.

Precautions

Obtain the phone number of the poison control center in your area—most centers have toll-free numbers—and keep it posted in a visible place in the kitchen and bathroom. Better yet, memorize the number. If your community has no poison control center, you can reach emergency service by dialing 9-1-1 or 0 for the operator.

Keep a one-ounce bottle of *syrup of ipecac* for each of your children. This is available at the pharmacy and is used to induce vomiting, should your child ingest something noxious. Also, keep *activated charcoal* to bind or deactivate poison and *Epsom salts* as a laxative. Use these products only on the instructions of a doctor or a trained professional at your local poison control center.

Poisons may be slow or fast acting. Learn the telltale signs of poisoning:

◆ An open container or poisonous plant materials near your ill child
◆ Nausea, vomiting, diarrhea
◆ Irregular breathing and slowed pulse
◆ Unusual body odor or breath
◆ Burns on the tongue and lips
◆ Drowsiness
◆ Unconsciousness
◆ Convulsions

What to Do in Case of Accidental Poisoning

1. If your child shows signs of poisoning, do not follow first-aid instructions printed on product labels. First, call your local poison control center or dial 9-1-1.

Be prepared to answer the following questions:

◆ What did the child take?
◆ What are the symptoms?
◆ How old is your child and what is her weight?
◆ How long since the poison was ingested?
◆ Does your child have any other health problems?
◆ Is she taking any other medications?
◆ What is your address and phone number?

2. If the poison was solid (pills, toadstools, mothballs), use a wet washcloth to wipe away any toxic remnants from the child's mouth.

3. On the advice of health professionals, give small sips of water or milk to dilute the poison if your child is conscious.

4. Don't make your child vomit unless the poison control center or doctor tells you to.

5. If you are trained in cardiopulmonary resuscitation (CPR) or first aid, administer rescue breathing or CPR, as the doctor recommends. But don't try emergency procedures if you've had no training.

6. Emergency personnel may have you call for an ambulance to transport your child to the hospital.

Store and Use Cleaning Supplies Safely

A s a class of poisons, household cleaning products can be especially dangerous because they are so accessible. Common sense tells us that cleaning supplies such as...

- Bleach
- Ammonia
- Window cleaners
- Surface degreasers (409, Fantastik)
- Scouring powder and pads
- Oven cleaners
- Drain openers
- Furniture polish and spray waxes
- Laundry and dishwasher detergent
- Silver, copper, and stainless steel polishes

should be kept out of youngsters' curious hands. According to the National Safety Council, in 1988, 10 percent of all calls to poison control centers were about accidents with such cleaning products.

Although many safety manuals stress that these potentially dangerous products should be locked away in childproof cabinets, others assert that it's safest to lock them in closets on shelves too high for your kids to reach, even if they stand on a chair. As some experts point out, if your bright youngster watches you unlatch a childproof device, sooner or later, she'll learn how to do it herself. *To be doubly safe, again, buy only products that come in childproof containers.*

Explain to your youngster that these cleaning products, if swallowed, can make him quite sick. Indeed, ingestion of some can prove fatal. *They are poisons!* Stress the consequences of tampering with these agents rather than simply saying it's "against the rules" to touch them. Kids always push the boundaries parents create. Rules, as they say, are made to be broken. But even a three-year-old will understand, "Don't touch! Big boo-boo!" or, "Big tummyache!"

Youngsters old enough to help with household chores should be taught how to properly use cleaning products. Supervise their use until you're satisfied that your child won't hurt himself in his eagerness to help. Teach him to direct window cleaner or other sprays away from the face and eyes and to avoid inhaling fumes from spray furniture polish. He should also wash his hands after touching cleaning agents—including detergents—and keep his hands away from his eyes until then. Only teenagers are mature enough to handle substances such as chlorine bleach, ammonia, oven cleaner (especially those containing lye), and drain opener—and then only with gloves and after they've read the label for safety guidelines.

Other Precautions

1. Make sure to store household cleaners in their original containers—avoid those that have contained food or drink. It's easy to forget or become confused.

2. Read all product safety labels, including what to do in case of accidents.

3. Never leave your young child alone around cleaning products. If you must stop dusting to answer the phone, take the spray polish or your child with you!

4. Use products only in accordance with instructions on the label. For example, mixing bleach and ammonia creates poisonous sulfuric acid gas. Other products are flammable.

5. Throw away products that have corroded or leaked through their containers.

6. If your child has skin or eye contact with a cleaning product, call the poison control center. Flush the skin or eye with warm running water for 15 minutes. (For eyes, wash from the nose outward.)

7. Make sure to store all cleaning products away from food.

8. If you're on vacation at a friend's or relative's home, be sure they observe the same safety precautions you use in your own home.

9. *If your child has swallowed one of these products or has been splashed in the eyes with them, call your local poison control center.* You might also want to refer to the previous section on poisons.

Monitor and Eliminate Radon Gas

R adon is an odorless, colorless radioactive gas that can percolate through the porous soil under your dwelling into your home. Radon forms during the natural breakdown of radium, a radioactive by-product of decaying uranium.

As radon itself decays, it releases radioactive "progeny," or "daughters." According to the Environmental Protection Agency (EPA), when these become trapped in the lungs, they "release small bursts of energy which can damage lung tissue and lead to lung cancer. It's like exposing your family to hundreds of chest X-rays each year."

In fact, the American Lung Association reports that radon is the second leading cause of lung cancer in the U.S. today. The EPA estimates that 5,000 to 20,000 lung cancer deaths each year are attributable to high concentrations of radon gas within the home. The risk increases with higher concentrations and greater durations of exposure. Smokers exposed to radon gas multiply their risk of lung cancer tenfold when compared to nonsmokers.

The EPA suspects that radon may be a problem in nearly every state. Approximately 4 million to 8 million homes have radon levels above those that are considered safe. About a million homes have twice the allowable level.

How Radon Gets into Your Home

Soil, minerals, and rocks such as granite, shale, phosphate, and pitchblende are natural sources of uranium and radon. Outdoors, radon can't accumulate in dangerous concentrations because of winds and constant air circulation. But when released into the soil, radon can leak into your home through cracks in its foundation or insulation, pipes, sumps, walls, atria, or other openings.

How Do You Know If You Have a Radon Problem?

Since you can't see, touch, smell, or hear radon, the only way to determine if this gas is present in dangerous levels in your home is to use a radon testing kit. The EPA recommends that all homeowners and tenants who live below the third floor should test their dwellings. Be aware that radon levels vary from house to house, so if your neighbor has little detectable radon, that doesn't mean that you can forgo testing your own home. Kits cost about $20 and are available by mail or from your local hardware store. Make sure they have an EPA or state seal of approval. Your state's Radon Office (see the Resource Guide for phone numbers) can provide you with a list of reliable test kits.

There are two types of do-it-yourself test kits: short-term and long-term. Short-term kits measure radon levels over a period of a few days to several months. After the allotted period of time, you mail the kit to its manufacturer, who then mails you the test results. Testers should be placed in the lowest living space within your house, with the doors and windows shut during the winter months. Long-term test kits take up to one year but are the most accurate means of testing. Radon levels can vary daily, monthly, or seasonally, depending on weather, ventilation, or the use of heating and air conditioning. Therefore, the longer the test period, the more accurate the results.

There are also one-day sampling tests that require a trained professional to come to your home. These tests are more expensive, averaging from $80 to $300, but give quick results. Your state Radon Office will have a list of qualified technicians (see the Resource Guide).

What You Should Do If You Find Radon in Your Home

The good news about radon is that its levels are easily reduced once detected. Most problems are corrected for between $200 and

$1,500. The American Lung Association offers the following suggestions:

◆ Ventilate your home thoroughly. Open windows and doors or use fans and heat exchangers to increase airflow.

◆ Make sure all crawl spaces under your home are vented.

◆ Seal any cracks in the foundation.

◆ Seal and vent the sump area.

◆ In serious cases, subslab ventilation may be required. This should be installed by a qualified contractor who is experienced in lowering radon levels and who has passed the EPA's National Radon Contractor Proficiency Exam. Contact your state's Radon Office for names.

◆ The EPA publishes *Radon Reduction Methods: A Homeowner's Guide* to help you remedy the problem yourself.

◆ Retest your home after you've remedied its structural problems.

Other Precautions

If you're in the market for a new home, you'll be better off to include radon testing prior to purchase in your inspection clause. Some states require sellers to disclose environmental hazards in their homes, if known to be present. The installation of a ventilation system may be a bargaining point. If the home you are purchasing had already been found to contain unsafe levels of radon, make sure any ventilation system that has been installed to mitigate the problem is in good working order. Ask the sellers for instructions on its proper maintenance.

Test for and Eliminate Lead

L ead is a highly toxic chemical that can accumulate in one's body over a lifetime. Lead poisoning can cause learning disabilities and chronic diseases of the nervous, cardiovascular, and reproductive systems as well as the kidneys. Children and fetuses are at greatest risk. Lead is a hidden hazard: It is found in paint, lead dust, soil, old pipes, dishes, and crystal. (By the way, pencil "lead" won't cause problems—it's really graphite. Rather, it's the paint coatings on pencils that children should not chew!)

According to the Public Health Service, as many as one out of every six children has blood lead levels above what is considered safe by the Centers for Disease Control. Other watchdog agencies, however, believe the problem is even more widespread. The Environmental Defense Fund, for example, estimates that nearly 75 percent of children between the ages of six months and five years living in New York City and 58 percent of those living in Los Angeles have unacceptable levels of lead in their blood.

Lead Paint, Dust, and Pipes

Lead-containing paint was banned in 1977, according to the Lead Institute, a national lead-hazard clearinghouse. Yet the Department of Housing and Urban Development estimates that 74 percent of all homes built before 1980 contain lead paint. Old furniture may have been painted or repainted with lead paint as well. Lead dust from cracking paint is easily ingested and can be tracked into your home. In addition, lead leaches into drinking water from corroded lead pipes and solder.

Precautions

1. Clean up. Vacuum carpets at least once a week. Wash floors, woodwork, and painted walls once a week with a gallon of warm water to which you've added one tablespoon of high-phosphate automatic *dishwashing* detergent. (The label should state the phosphate content.) Your child should always wash his hands before eating, and don't let him eat anything that has fallen to the floor. *Moreover, never allow your child to eat or suck on lead paint or painted surfaces. Treat it as a poison.*

2. Don't remove lead paint yourself. Sanding, scraping, or burning off lead paint releases harmful dust and debris. Call a professional de-leading contractor. Keep out of your home during lead-paint removal. Make sure floors, walls, and other surfaces have been washed thoroughly before moving back in.

3. Be aware of lead hazards in your child's hobbies. Solder, paints, and ceramic glazes can contain lead. Handwashing is essential after handling these products.

4. Eat wisely. Calcium, iron, and vitamin C help your child's body fight lead. Dairy products, such as milk, yogurt, and cheese, are an excellent calcium source. Iron-rich foods include lean beef, dark green and leafy vegetables, water-packed tuna, raisins, eggs, and peanuts. Citrus fruits, tomatoes, and potatoes supply vitamin C. All of these foods should be in the family's diet. What's more, fats bind with lead and keep the substance in your body, which is one more good reason to cut down on fatty or fried foods: chips, bacon, butter, fried chicken, and fatty meats. (More on nutrition in 40, Develop Healthful Eating Habits.)

5. Protect your drinking water. If your home has old, corroding pipes, you might consider retrofitting your plumbing. If that's impossible, make sure to allow the tap to run for a full two minutes before using the water to drink or cook. Observe this rule especially carefully first thing in the morning, after water has been sitting in the pipes all night. Never use hot tap water for cooking or drinking. Lead might have leached into the water while standing in the pipes all night.

6. Recognize the signs of lead poisoning. Because lead poisoning can develop slowly, its symptoms may be hard to detect. In addition, they often mimic those of the flu:

Stomachaches and headaches
Loss of appetite
Irritability
Lethargy and loss of desire to play

7. If you're worried about your child's exposure, have your doctor test his blood for lead. Be sure to request a *direct lead* test, as the earlier indirect testing proved highly inaccurate in measuring lead levels. If the results show a high level of lead, other tests and exams may be required. Your doctor will be able to offer advice—and possibly prescribe medications—to help limit the effects of lead poisoning.

Dishes

Much attention has been devoted lately to the problem of lead in dishes and crystal, and for good reason. Long-term exposure to lead in dishes can result in lead poisoning. Unfortunately, without a manufacturer's disclosure or a home test kit, you can't tell which dishes are suspect. Simply looking at them won't suffice. The china pattern, country in which it was manufactured, color, or price is not significant; the glaze, however, is. You can't wash the problem away, either, because the lead leaches out of the glaze slowly, over a long period of time. (Stoneware is safer since it's usually coated with a non-lead film.)

In 1991, the state of California sued the following 10 china manufacturers to force them to warn consumers of lead hazards in their products:

Wedgwood	Noritake
Lenox	Villeroy & Boch
Mikasa	Pickard
Royal Doulton	Pfaltzgraff
Fitz & Floyd	Syracuse China

Some dishes from the list above have high lead levels, while others have relatively small amounts that nevertheless exceed stringent California standards. You should also know, however, that the

California Attorney General's office has compiled a list of hundreds of china patterns that meet the state's standards. For a copy, send a self-addressed, stamped envelope (two stamps) to:

> Office of the Attorney General
> Press Office
> 1515 K Street
> Sacramento, CA 95814

Precautions

How can you protect your family from the dangers of lead in dishes? First, identify and avoid using high-risk items. These are:

- **Old china:** Don't eat from heirlooms inherited from an earlier generation, which might have been manufactured before lead was a recognized hazard.
- **Handcrafted ceramics:** You may be unable to determine whether the artisan used lead-free glazes and whether the pottery was fired in high-temperature kilns.
- **Decorated and multicolored inside surfaces:** Watch for decorations that come in contact with food.
- **Decoration painted over glaze:** You can feel this with your finger.
- **Corroded glaze:** A dusty or chalky gray residue will be present even after you've washed the plate.

If you've identified questionable china dishes, avoid:

1. Storing food or drink in them. Be especially cautious of foods such as tomatoes, citrus and other fruit juices, wine, salsa, applesauce, coffee, tea, colas, and vinaigrettes, which have a high acid content that can strip off lead. The longer the storage period, the more lead will leach into the food.

2. Serving acidic foods on these dishes.

3. Using these as your everyday china.

4. Heating or microwaving in them. Heat speeds the leaching process.

5. Storing wine in leaded-crystal decanters.

To ensure your family's safety, check for lead content with the manufacturer or use a lead-testing kit. (See the Resource Guide for phone numbers.)

The Lead Institute is a resource for EPA and Consumers Union-approved lead-testing kits as well as labs that detect the substance in paint, soil, dishes, solder, dust, crystal, pipes, and water. Kits cost about $30 and are available through the Lead Institute.

Dishes made of glass (but not lead crystal) are safe if they are unpainted, as are stoneware and lead-free or low-lead china. The Hall China Company and Corning Ware sell lead-free china. Otherwise, check with manufacturers if you're contemplating trading in your old china for a new pattern.

Find the Best Babysitter and Nanny

The psychological thriller *The Hand That Rocks the Cradle* certainly made a lot of parents nervous—and understandably so! Nothing is more precious to us than our children. One of our most important parental responsibilities is finding trustworthy caregivers who will love, respect, and watch over our youngsters as carefully as we do.

How to Find a Good Sitter

1. Be clear about your needs. Are you looking for someone to cover for you on a Saturday night, or do you need a live-in nanny who will become "part of the family"? In either case, you will need to decide if you want the caregiver to:

◆ Do household chores
◆ Play with and stimulate your youngsters
◆ Feed and bathe them
◆ Drive your children to appointments and lessons
◆ Help out with homework

Determine how much you're willing to pay and the hours you'll need the sitter to work. Do you need a certified nanny, an au pair, a teenage boy to play with your son, or a grandma who will cuddle your baby?

2. Network. According to the National Center for Missing and Exploited Children, the best child-care recommendations come from family, friends, and neighbors. They know your children and needs and have your best interest at heart. Barring that, you can advertise in local high school or college newspapers and leave notices

at your church, synagogue, play group, or park. Nursing students at
a local college can make excellent sitters, especially since they're car-
ing people who are trained in first aid and CPR.

Child-care agencies can speed your search because they screen
potential applicants for you, but you might want to choose an
agency as meticulously as you would a sitter. Since there are no
national standards for such agencies, find out how long the company has been in business and ask for references. In addition, ask what
standards it requires of its caregivers. Even if the agency boasts that
it's bonded (meaning it has insurance that will cover certain losses,
such as theft), that doesn't protect your child! Ask if the agency has
done a criminal-record check on potential employees. Also, pay
attention to how the agency treats you. The more questions the personnel ask of you, the more likely they are to carefully screen and
select candidates, too.

You will have to pay the agency a fee (often four weeks of the
caregiver's salary) for a sitter obtained in this manner, so check for
complaints at the Better Business Bureau and inquire what percentage of the agency's placements last more than a year.

3. Screen carefully. In a phone interview, ask the candidate
about her experience: how many years she has worked, the ages and
genders of children she has watched, the duration of previous jobs,
and why she left. Be suspicious of unexplained gaps in her employment history. Ask for three references from former employers. If
these are not forthcoming, seek another sitter. Check references carefully. Don't simply rely on letters of recommendation. Call former
employers. If they seem evasive or vague, chances are that they were
dissatisfied with the sitter. You can even ask your local FBI or sher-
iff's office to conduct a nationwide criminal check for a fee of about
$15, though you will need the candidate's permission.

During the in-person interview, watch how the candidate reacts
to your child when he's irritable or demanding. Ask how she would
respond to hypothetical situations such as emergencies or tantrums.
Does she seem comfortable around kids? Does she have any hearing,
vision, or other health problems that might impair her ability to
respond quickly? What are her attitudes toward discipline? Have the

candidate fill out a job application (see Resource Guide) in which she must list references, her current phone number and address, and her employment history.

4. Delineate duties. Make your expectations clear regarding responsibilities, hours, salary, visitors for both the sitter and your child (in the case of teenage sitters, experts recommend no visitors), vacation (for live-ins), and so on.

5. Try a probationary period. After you've narrowed the field to one or two candidates, ask each to spend some paid time with your family. A few hours may be adequate for a teenager who'll be watching your child on Saturday nights, but you might want to spend a weekend with a potential live-in. This way, you can observe how the sitter interacts with your family and determine whether you feel comfortable with her. Trust your intuition.

Precautions

If you're just heading out for a Saturday night on the town, ask the sitter to arrive 15 minutes early to acquaint herself with your household and kids. Introduce her to your youngsters and explain to them that the sitter will be in charge during your absence.

Even if your sitter is a live-in, leave a list with the following information:

- ◆ Where you will be and how you can be reached.
- ◆ Your address (with zip code) and phone number (with area code), in case she must direct emergency vehicles to your home.
- ◆ Your pediatrician's or doctor's phone number.
- ◆ The number of a neighbor, friend, or close relative.
- ◆ Police department number.
- ◆ Fire department number.
- ◆ Poison control center number.

Take the sitter on a tour inside and outside the home and point out potential danger spots. Show her where you keep the fire extinguishers and first-aid equipment. Discuss family rules regarding bedtime, snacks, homework, and TV. If she must administer medication, explain the dosage and procedure. Make sure that she:

- Locks all outside doors after you leave.
- Keeps the children away from potentially hazardous substances and situations.
- Tells phone callers you're "busy right now," rather than announcing your absence.
- Doesn't open the door to anyone, including her friends.
- Keeps her own phone calls short and sweet.

If you're using a new teenage sitter, it's wise to call in as the evening progresses, just to check on how your family is doing.

Teach Your Child Latchkey Safety

Accordingto recent surveys by the Bureau of Labor Statistics, nearly 75 percent of all married mothers in this country with school-age children are employed. Most families provide child care, but sometimes circumstances, such as economic hardship, require that a child be left alone while his parents are at work. Indeed, Child Care Action Campaign, a child-care advocacy group, estimates that 25 percent of school-age children are left on their own after school. Although the hit movie *Home Alone* made it seem as if staying in the house by oneself is a lark, most children must adjust to being left alone. For some it can be a difficult transition. It's up to you to help your child make the adjustment safely.

Most authorities believe children should not be left alone until the age of 10 or 11 (and never for more than two to three hours). Kids younger than that have not yet developed the ability to reason abstractly and come up with solutions to difficult problems.

Whether or not your child is well-suited to being home alone depends on his maturity. To help determine if your youngster can handle it, ask yourself the following questions:

- ◆ How does he carry out household responsibilities?
- ◆ Is he careful?
- ◆ Does he pay attention to details?
- ◆ How responsible is he about school obligations or religious activities?
- ◆ How does he respond to crises?
- ◆ Do you feel you can trust his judgment?

A destructive or impulsive child should not be left alone.

Preparing Your Child to Be Left Alone

Organizations such as the YMCA, Girl Scouts, Campfire Girls, and Boy Scouts give safety and "On My Own" workshops for kids. If at all possible, enroll your youngster in one of these to help him prepare for emergency situations. Books such as *The Parent/Child Manual on Latchkey Kids* by Charlene Solomon as well as videotapes can help you and your youngster learn about safety and possible responses to crises.

Make sure to keep lines of communication open between the two of you. If your youngster is usually able to share his feelings with you, he'll be more likely to come to you when he's feeling embarrassed or upset about an incident that occurred while he was on his own. Make sure to talk with your child about any new arrangements and have him practice reciting his phone number (with area code), address (including the city and state), your work number, and other emergency procedures such as dialing 9-1-1, the poison control center, or 0 for the operator. Develop a routine in which he will check in with you or a trusted neighbor as soon as he walks in the door. Make time for additional phone contact during the afternoon.

Try role playing: Ask your youngster how he would respond if:
◆ There were a power failure.
◆ He lost his house key.
◆ Someone rang the doorbell.
◆ He came home to find the front door open.
◆ Someone followed him home from school.
◆ He became frightened by creaking noises in the house.
◆ A fire started.

You can think of many more potentially dangerous or frightening situations. Never belittle his response, but guide him toward the safest options.

It might be helpful to do several trial runs by stepping out to a friend's house. Begin with a 30-minute visit. The following week, expand to 40 minutes, and so on. Before you go, review the safety rules you've established and leave the phone number of where you'll be and the number of a neighbor or relative. Also, make sure your child has access to a first-aid kit.

Safety Rules

It's important to establish safety rules before you leave. Go over these rules with your child:

- Keep your key hidden, either pinned to your pants pocket or around your neck on a chain that's tucked into your shirt. (You don't want to advertise to strangers that you'll be home alone.)
- Learn your name, address (including city and state), phone number (including area code), and our work numbers by heart.
- Never talk to strangers or accept offers of candy or rides. Just because an adult knows your name or looks familiar doesn't mean he's your friend. (See 24, Help Your Child Deal with Strangers, and 28, Prevent Sexual Abuse.)
- If someone other than a close friend or relative asks to take your picture or wants you to keep a secret, run away and tell us right away.
- If you feel you're being followed by a stranger, don't go home to an empty house. Instead, go to a neighbor's house (one that has a "Neighborhood Watch" sticker on the window may also do), a store, the police station, or any place that's well lit and has lots of people.
- Never enter the house if the door or windows are open or broken.
- Don't cook, invite friends over, or go to a friend's house without our permission.
- If you think you've swallowed poison or gotten some in your eyes or on your skin, call the poison control center.
- If you lose your key, there's one hidden in the garage (or at a neighbor's).
- Always call to check in when you've gotten home.
- If a fire starts, don't try to put it out yourself. Get out of the house and call the fire department (or 9-1-1) from a neighbor's house.

◆ If you're scared, you can always call us at work.
◆ Always let us know if something upsetting or embarrassing happened while we were gone.

When You Return

Make sure to spend time talking with your child after work. Ask
him if anything unusual occurred in your absence. Let him know
that you care about his concerns and fears. If your child shows such
signs of stress as destructive behavior; marked changes in school per-
formance or friendships; or headaches, stomachaches, and sleep or
appetite disturbances that are unrelated to illness, you should investigate further. *If you find your child is too fearful, angry, or depressed,
seek out other afterschool child-care alternatives.*

While a latchkey arrangement may not be appropriate for all
children, taking these precautions can make the experience as safe as
possible for your child.

Practice Swimming Pool Safety

ome swimming pools can be great fun, but they're also awash with potential for disaster. Drowning is the second most common cause of accidental death for children under the age of 14. Near-drownings can cause permanent brain damage. The following tips will help you keep your child safe around your or your neighbor's pool:

◆ Children should never swim without an adult present.

◆ Not even older children should swim alone. A buddy can go for help should the need arise.

◆ No diving from the shallow end of the pool.

◆ No running around the pool decking. It may be slippery when wet.

◆ No swimming during inclement weather and especially not during thunderstorms.

◆ Neighborhood children are not allowed in the pool if you aren't present.

◆ Keep glassware, glass bottles of suntan lotion or drinks, and other breakable items away from the pool area.

◆ Keep a life preserver or flotation jacket (not an inflatable toy) and a rescue pole in close proximity to the pool.

◆ Install a phone outside near the pool.

◆ Some states require in-ground pools to be surrounded on all sides with a fence five feet high or taller. These fences should have self-closing, self-latching gates. (Make sure the latch is well out of reach of young children—4 1/2 feet from the ground.) Even if it's not required in your state, a fence is a good idea. Never use one wall of your house as a substitute for a fence—especially if that wall has a door or sliding glass window that opens onto the pool area. (That defeats the purpose of the fence.)

◆ Take toys and floats out of the pool when it's not in use. These attract children.

◆ Completely cover your pool when it's not in use. According to the National Safety Council, children and adults have become trapped and have drowned in partially covered pools.

◆ Give your youngsters swimming lessons. If they've had no problem with frequent ear infections, you might consider lessons when they're three years old. At the very least, they should know how to swim over to the side of the pool, hang on, and call for help if they have fallen into the water. No matter how good the instruction, however, lessons do not prevent a child from drowning.

◆ Learn rescue breathing and CPR. (See 37, Learn Rescue Breathing, CPR, and the Heimlich Maneuver for more details.) You might even consider taking a Red Cross water safety or life-saving course.

◆ Discourage your child from playing near bodies of water. There is always the danger of falling in!

For more safety tips regarding public pools and other bodies of water, refer to 33, Watch for Playground Safety.

Keep Play Equipment Safe

First, a few statistics. You and your child have approximately 150,000 toys to choose from! That's how many playthings are on the market today. Yet, according to the Product Safety Commission, toys and home playground equipment injure about 200,000 people a year. Some 40 percent of these injuries (80,000) are serious enough to require hospital emergency-room treatment. Children under 10 account for about 50 percent of all toy-related mishaps.

How to Protect Your Child

1. Choose appropriate toys. Make sure the toy you're considering for purchase is suitable for your neighborhood. You might not want to purchase a skateboard if you live in a hilly community that has no sidewalks, for example.

Different children mature at varying rates. Your neighbor's six-year-old may be ready for roller skates while your first-grader may not. Your selection of suitable playthings depends on your child's interests and development. You can, however, follow some general, age-appropriate guidelines.

Preschoolers (ages three to five). These youngsters are developing social skills and motor coordination. They play in groups, dart around the playground, climb jungle gyms, ride tricycles or Big Wheels, string beads, color and paint, build with blocks, examine ant hills, play act, and dress up. Some may even begin to read.

Preschoolers' toys must be sturdy enough to take a beating. They should be constructed of unbreakable, nontoxic materials that have no sharp or rough edges. Scissors should have blunt ends, clay should be edible—though not delicious (a mixture of flour, water, salt, and food coloring works best), and vehicles should be low to the ground (to avoid tipping). The Consumer Federation of America recommends that platforms and slides for preschoolers' jungle gyms not exceed six feet in height.

Primary School Children (ages six to eight). These children often play in groups of same-gender friends. They engage in make-believe play (house, superheroes, school) and learn how to cooperate. Primary-school–age children may be ready for roller skates and two-wheelers with training wheels. (See 20, Insist on Bicycle Safety.) Arts and crafts, model building, woodworking, and simple science experiments (and kits) may require parental involvement, if not direct supervision. Darts, arrows, and other target toys should have Velcro or suction-cup tips. Jungle gyms for school-age youngsters should be no taller than seven feet.

Midrange Children (ages nine to twelve). These youngsters are becoming more independent and individualized. They get involved in team and individual sports, electronic and computer games, crafts, dramatic play, and hobbies. Children of this age will enjoy the freedom that comes with bikes, skateboards, or roller skates. They may become engrossed in chemistry sets and microscopes as well as radios and cassette players. Supervise their play with these toys along with such toys as darts or arrows.

2. Make sure your child understands the rules. Before your youngster begins playing with a new toy, review its proper use with her. Point out potentially dangerous misuses, such as throwing sandbox sand at a playmate's eyes. It's important to enforce the rule that there's no standing on or jumping from swing-set swings. If your youngster likes to play with chemistry sets, make sure she doesn't mix household substances with those that came with the kit. It's also a good idea to keep older siblings' toys away from younger brothers and sisters who could become hurt playing with them. Outdoor toys should not be played with inside the house.

3. Maintain toys properly. Even the "safest" toys in the world can present a danger if used when they are broken or improperly maintained. If you have a jungle gym in the backyard, check it weekly to ensure that no sharp bolts can scrape your child. Look for rust, splinters, and sharp edges. Bicycles need to be checked periodically, too. Is the chain tight? Are the handlebars on firmly? Has your child outgrown the current seat setting? Inspect wiring and battery compartments on electrical toys. If you must repair a toy, don't alter it in any way that would negate safety features. When in doubt, throw the toy out!

4. Store toys properly. Toy boxes have proven to be real dangers for young children who climb in, only to have the lid shut on them. (Fingers can be pinched, but, worse, the child could suffocate within.) The National Safety Council suggests using lightweight chests that have large ventilation holes. Otherwise, using low shelves as storage space is your best bet. Help your preschooler and primary-school-age child learn how to put away her toys. Little is more unpleasant than stepping on a set of jacks, a marble collection, or a roller skate in the middle of the night! Make cleanup time a game as you work together.

Some Special Precautions

Repainted Toys

Hand-me-down toys can be great, but beware that old toys may have been refinished with lead-containing paint. A child who sucks or chews on such a toy could suffer lead poisoning, so throw away any suspect toys. If you're inclined to repaint toys, make sure the paint is lead-free.

Electric Toys

Toys that run on ordinary house current should be approved by independent safety-testing companies like Underwriters Laboratories (UL). Look for the seal. Battery operated toys and those with low-voltage transformers are safer. Teach your children that they should never touch electric toys (or appliances) if their hands or bodies are wet. And, as stated above, check regularly for faulty wiring.

Kites and Balloons

Teach your youngsters to fly their kites away from power lines, since serious shock can result if the kite becomes entangled in them. It's also unwise to fly a kite during a rainstorm (Ben Franklin notwithstanding) because of the possibility of being struck by lightning.

Helium-filled balloons, especially Mylar ones, also pose a danger of electric shock, even fire, if they become entangled in power lines. They should not leave your household. Moreover, be aware that simple rubber balloons can be dangerous playthings for preschoolers, who may inhale them while trying to blow them up. Even balloon fragments have caused children to choke.

Home Playground Equipment

Tests by the federal Consumer Product Safety Commission (CPSC) have found that a six-inch-deep layer of uncompressed, fine, dry sand beneath a jungle gym can protect against injury from a fall of five feet. (Of course depending on how a child falls, injury can occur no matter what the precautions.) Both the CPSC and the nonprofit Consumer Federation of America recommend establishing a deep (at least nine inches) layer of wood chips, mulch, or bark, which should be raked and supplemented regularly to maintain its resilience. Lawn or regular dirt beneath a jungle gym can become compacted and hard. Under no circumstances should you position a jungle gym on a concrete or other paved surface that can lead to serious injury in the event your child falls.

The National Safety Council suggests the following home jungle gym precautions:
- Be sure to place the jungle gym on level ground.
- Anchor it well.
- The play set should be well away from fences, hedges, or buildings: Passing children might otherwise be forced to walk too close to moving swings in order to pass by.
- Be sure bolts are protected by "acorn" nuts or are filed smooth.
- Remove and replace jagged sheet metal.

- ◆ S-hooks should be bent closed, or children might catch their clothes or fingers in them.
- ◆ Inspect the jungle gym once a week. Be sure it remains stable, and watch for wear, rust, rot, and other signs of deterioration.

Be Sure Electrical Outlets, Wires, and Switches Are Safe

People in the childproofing business warn parents to expect the unexpected. That can hold doubly true when it comes to electrical outlets, wires, and switches. Preschoolers, with their highly developed curiosity, might decide to probe a wall socket with a nail or a safety pin. A school-age child might want to perform a science experiment: "If I put this wire in the socket, will my electric buzzer ring?"

As we know, such research can prove fatal. The following suggestions can help you avoid typical hazards associated with electrical outlets, wires, and switches.

- Cover electrical outlets with receptacle covers (sold in most grocery stores).
- Replace any damaged power cords.
- Avoid using "octopus" outlets, which can overload circuits.
- Don't run power cords under carpeting, where they can become worn and frayed.
- Extension cords should be heavy enough to handle the appliances that are plugged into them.
- Never remove the third grounding prong from an electrical plug.
- Never hang wires from nails. New electrical fixtures should be "hard wired."
- Know the location of your fuse box or circuit breakers. Label circuit breakers and fuses in case of emergency.
- Keep spare fuses handy and never replace a fuse with the wrong amperage.

◆ Make sure that your house wiring can handle the load you've placed on it.
◆ Kitchen islands with garbage-disposal switches within reach of children can pose special dangers. Cover these with switch guards.

Check Electrical Appliances

Observe the following precautions with home electrical appliances:

◆ Teach your child how to use (and not use) the appliances you've permitted her to touch. As a child, I once attempted to make a grilled cheese sandwich by stuffing a piece of bread and a slice of cheese down the slot of a pop-up toaster. No one had told me it couldn't be done beforehand! Expect the unexpected.

◆ Explain to your youngster the danger of touching any appliances with wet hands or a wet body.

◆ Keep electrical appliances such as radios and hair dryers out of the bathroom whenever possible. And always keep them well away from water, unplugging them when not in use (or use battery-operated appliances such as electric toothbrushes).

◆ Teach your school-age child how to shut off the circuit breaker and unscrew fuses, should an emergency arise.

◆ Teach your child to unplug an appliance that smokes or shoots off sparks. In case she may not be able to unplug it, she should know how to unscrew the fuse and/or shut off the circuit breaker.

◆ Remove the doors of any abandoned refrigerators and freezers. Old-fashioned refrigerators and freezers have latch closures that can entrap children hiding within, causing them to suffocate.

◆ Washers and dryers should be properly grounded. If you are unsure how to do this, refer to the instruction manuals or call a local dealer.

◆ Never leave a hot iron unattended.

- Teach your youngsters to keep hands as well as breakable and metal items out of such potentially dangerous appliances as blenders, mixers, food processors, garbage disposals, juice extracters, and trash compacters.
- Instruct your preschooler to keep away from your stereo and VCR equipment. (Young children are apt to experiment by putting objects in welcoming slots. Safety catalogues sell VCR locks. See Resource Guide.) If you allow your school-age child to operate the TV, stereo, or VCR, be sure she understands how you want these appliances treated.
- Don't allow your youngster to use your computer without your supervision until you feel she has mastered its operation.
- Save all appliance operating manuals. Store them in a spare drawer in the kitchen or utility room.
- Unplug and store power tools such as drills, saws, and lathes well out of reach. If you want to teach your youngster how to operate these tools, you must supervise constantly. Never remove safety guards or shields.
- Night-lights may be helpful, but keep them well away from draperies, bedding, or other materials that may catch fire. Instruct your youngsters never to drape scarves or other fabric or paper items over lamps and lampshades.
- Teach your child to wait until a light bulb has cooled down before changing it.
- Keep portable heaters at least three feet away from drapes, bedding, walls, or other flammable materials.
- When teaching your youngster how to use a microwave oven, remind her never to place metal objects or dishes decorated with gold or other metal designs in the oven. (More on microwave safety in 13, Practice Safety in the Kitchen.) To make sure your oven is not leaking dangerous waves, have an authorized repair person test it.
- Immediately replace or repair any electrical appliance that no longer functions perfectly.
- All electrical appliances in your home should bear the UL seal of approval.

Drink Purified Water

By some estimates, over 700 contaminants foul the U.S. water supply.

- Microbes and various bacteria and viruses can seep in from incorrectly placed, constructed, or maintained septic tanks and cause diseases such as dysentery and giardiasis.
- Minerals and metals: Unsafe levels of fluoride can cause bone disease in both adults and children, and nitrate can cause brain damage, even death, in infants.
- Lead from old pipes or solder can cause lead poisoning, and children are particularly vulnerable. (See 4, Test for and Eliminate Lead.)
- Radioactive material, such as radon, has infiltrated water in deep, private wells and can cause cancer (see 3, Monitor and Eliminate Radon Gas) once it is released in the home.
- Volatile organic compounds like paint and paint thinner, benzene, gasoline, and industrial and dry-cleaning solvents can poison your water supply and cause cancer and leukemia.
- Organic chemicals like pesticides and chemical fertilizers can seep into groundwater and cause cancer.

The prospect of contamination with these agents is frightening but you can protect your family by taking certain precautions.

Water Testing

Water supplies of any drinking water systems serving more than 25 homes are required to be analyzed for contaminants, with the test results being made available to consumers. Write to your city, county, or state water agency for details.

If you have reason to believe that your drinking water is unsafe, or if you are buying a home that has a private well or septic system, you may want to have your water analyzed. The EPA has a drinking water hotline (listed in the Resource Guide.) Since different areas of the country have different contaminants to worry about, the EPA line helps you ascertain which should be of concern to you. Your state water agency may have lab recommendations as well. Some states even provide water testing for free or for a minimal fee.

Lead-testing kits can determine if your drinking water contains dangerous levels of lead.

Purifying Your Water

According to *Consumer Reports,* about 10 million homes in the United States have water purifying systems. There are systems that purify the entire water supply to your home and others that attach to individual faucets, refrigerator water dispensers, and showers. You can rent a system on a monthly basis from a water-softening service, or install your own. Systems range in price from about $59 to over $1,000, depending on your needs.

Here are the most commonly used water purification systems:

Activated Carbon: This system uses a carbon filter that removes volatile organic compounds and organic chemicals as well. (I have one of these installed on my refrigerator water and ice dispensing line.) The filter needs changing at least once a year.

Water Softener: Sodium or potassium chloride tablets filter excess calcium, magnesium, and several toxic metals as well as radium from the water. Water-softening companies rent tanks for a small monthly fee.

Reverse Osmosis: Water passes through an

extremely fine membrane that filters out dirt and
larger chemical molecules.

Distillation: Water is boiled in one container, and a
separate clean container captures and condenses the
steam. Although minerals and solid contaminants
remain in the first container, the distilled water
must be further purified by an activated-carbon filter to remove liquid organic contaminants.

Aeration System: This device is installed on the
water main leading into the house to filter out
radon.

Any home water-treatment system you purchase should have
received the Water Quality Association or the National Sanitation
Foundation seal of approval. These groups set standards and test systems.

If all else fails, you can always buy bottled drinking water. In
some states, this is available in 5- or 10-gallon dispensers.

Prevent Falls

According to the National Safe Kids Campaign, a child-safety advocacy group, of all childhood injuries, falls are the leading cause of hospitalization and emergency room visits. That stands to reason: Kids constantly explore their environment to learn about the world around them. While they climb, run, and jump, the potential to fall is always present. You may be unable to control falls that occur at school or on the playground, but you can do much to keep your child safe from falls in your home. The following tips will guide you:

- If your child is old enough to retrieve items from upper kitchen cabinets, insist that he use a sturdy stepping stool. A chair can easily tip over and a drawer can collapse under his weight.
- To prevent falls from windows, install window guards. According to the National Safe Kids Campaign, an unguarded window that is opened only five inches is hazardous to a child under the age of 10; screens aren't sturdy enough to hold a child in. When installing window guards, however, be sure not to block windows that open to fire escapes.
- Furniture should not be pushed against a window. That would give your youngster easy access.
- Never leave young children alone on high decks, terraces, fire escapes, or balconies. Make sure that the railings which surround these structures are sturdy and that their slats lie sufficiently close together to prevent your child from pushing through.
- Wipe up any spilled liquid immediately so your youngster won't slip on it.

◆ Safeguard against falls in the bathroom. (See 14, Practice Safety in the Bathroom, for tips on how to do so.)

◆ Insist that your youngster clean up his toys after playing with them that day. It's easy for children and adults alike to trip and fall on toys scattered about. (Marbles and roller skates are probably the worst offenders.)

◆ If your kids have bunk beds, take special precautions:

  ◆ Make sure that all openings are small and that the sturdy wood slats, metal straps, or wires that are bolted onto the bed frame firmly support the mattresses.

  ◆ The National Safety Council specifies that the top of the upper guardrail should be at least five inches above the top of the mattress. Make sure it's securely fastened to the bed frame.

  ◆ Ladders should be in perfect condition and secured to the bed frame.

  ◆ Beds are not trampolines or jungle gyms! Don't allow your kids to roughhouse, hang from, or jump on their beds, especially upper bunks.

  ◆ Children younger than six should not sleep in upper bunks.

Practice Safety in the Kitchen

ost families spend a large proportion of their time preparing meals, conversing, eating, and even entertaining in the kitchen. Kids feel warm and comfortable in the kitchen—there's nothing like the smell of baking cookies to bring them running. But, inviting as the kitchen may be, it is one of two rooms in the home (the other being the bathroom) that pose special dangers. What follows are some kitchen safety tips.

Scalds and Burns

According to the National Safe Kids Campaign, hot liquids—not fire—are the most common cause of young children's burns. Here are some hints to keeping your child safe:

- Turn your water heater thermostat down to "low," "warm," or 120°F. That's hot enough for cleaning dishes, even in the dishwasher, without risking scalding your child. (Besides, it saves energy!)
- Turn pan handles toward the back of the stove or parallel with the edge of the stove. Never allow them to hang over, where a child can grab them.
- Keep hot food and drink away from the edges of tables or counters, where young children may reach for them. Until your child is in kindergarten, avoid using tablecloths. Youngsters can yank on these, pulling hot foods down on themselves.
- Never carry your child and hot liquid or food at the same time.

- Keep your child away from the stove when you're cooking—especially if you're frying spattery foods.
- Keep pot holders close to the stove, and don't use kitchen towels or aprons—they can catch fire.
- If at all possible, choose a stove with controls out of young children's reach. Some stoves have safety covers that hide the knobs.
- Shield your child from steam. It burns as quickly as boiling water. Lift pot lids *away* from your faces and bodies.

Knives

Children tend to have a certain fascination with knives. To keep that fascination from turning into trouble, here are some keen suggestions:

- Teach your youngster a healthy respect for knives.
- Keep knives in a special rack or compartment. If they're kept in a drawer, make sure it has been equipped with a childproofing device.
- Show your child how to cut bread, rolls, and the like away from his hands and body.

Fire

Kitchen fires are commonplace, but they can be avoided. Observe the following precautions:

- Keep matches in closed containers locked out of your youngster's reach in childproof cabinets.
- If you allow your child to cook, make sure he wears short sleeves. Long sleeves can catch fire and can snag on pot handles.
- Dish towels and pot holders should be hung away from the stove and oven. Left near a flame, they risk catching fire.
- Teach your youngster that he should never throw water on a grease fire—that only makes it worse. Instead, he should:
  - Turn off the burner,
  - Slide a lid or even a cookie sheet over the pan to cut off oxygen,
  - Leave the pan in place until it cools to room temperature.

- If a fire should erupt in the oven broiler, he should shut off the heat and keep the door closed until the flames die from lack of oxygen. (Opening the door will only feed them.)
- If a fire starts in the toaster or toaster-oven, unplug the appliance. Only adults should try to remove the burning object, and they should use a *wooden* utensil.
- Never throw water on a plugged-in electric appliance that's emitting sparks or flames. Doing so can deliver a powerful electrical shock.
- Keep a fire extinguisher in the kitchen—show your child where it is and how to use it—and recharge it yearly.
- Develop a fire safety plan for your family. (See Part VI, Fire Awareness.)

Microwave Safety

In general, today's microwave ovens are safe. They must meet exacting standards set by the Department of Health and Human Services. But just because the unit is safe doesn't mean that it's being used safely. The following guidelines will protect your child from injuries due to microwave use. He should be well versed in these if he's going to use the microwave in your absence.

- Use proper microwave utensils.
  - Use glass or china dinnerware without metal trim. Corning Ware, clay pots, Pyrex, paper (excluding Chinese take-out containers that have metal handles), and plastic pans, plates, and bowls are all acceptable.
  - Never use foil in the microwave. Metal interferes with the absorption of microwaves, can cause sparks, and may start a fire.
  - Foil-lined or -wrapped containers are not recommended. Whenever your child is heating anything, including a packaged frozen dinner, make sure the container is microwave safe.
  - Never leave a metal spoon, fork, or knife in or on any dish that you're microwaving.
  - Metal pots, pans, and pie pans, pewter, and silver serv-

ing pieces are not recommended for microwave use.

◆ Food covers should be vented to allow steam to escape. You can do this by either poking holes in the cover or leaving a gap somewhere between the cover and the dish.

◆ Use pot holders to remove cooked foods.

◆ Never run the microwave without food in it. Don't use it as a timer.

◆ Never cook or reheat eggs in their shells in the microwave. They can explode.

◆ Don't overcook foods. Potatoes, for example, can catch fire if cooked too long in the microwave. In case of fire, pull out the plug and leave the door shut until the lack of oxygen has suffocated the flames.

◆ It's best to use the minimum cooking time recommended. You can always add more time (watching carefully) if need be. Also, keep in mind that microwaved foods continue cooking after you've removed them from the oven: Be careful to test their heat before you or your child takes a bite.

◆ Foods cooked in the microwave heat unevenly, so stir them to distribute the heat before eating. Give solid foods a half- or quarter-turn at appropriate intervals. Observe the recommended "standing time" on product packages and in recipes.

◆ Recently, concern has been expressed about the possibility of dangerous chemicals leaching from plastic wrap into foods microwaved at high temperatures. To play it safe, use waxed paper or a microwave-safe vented plastic dome sold in houseware departments to cover foods as they cook. (This makes environmental sense, too, since the dome is reusable.)

◆ When removing any covering from microwaved foods, allow steam to escape safely by cutting vents in the cover or lifting the lid away from the face and body.

◆ Never put food that is still in the can or pop corn (unless in utensils or bags specifically designed for microwave use) in the microwave, nor should you heat or dry nonfood-related items in it. This applies to conventional ovens, too.

◆ Make sure your unit is safe. To help keep it safe:

◆ Never tamper or interfere with the safety latches.

◆ Never try to operate the oven with the door open.

◆ Make sure sealing surfaces are clean and that nothing interferes with their ability to keep microwaves inside the oven.

◆ Never operate the oven if it's broken or if the door, hinges, or latches are damaged. Call an authorized, qualified repair person to fix the unit.

◆ Your authorized repair person can check the unit for microwave leaks.

General Kitchen Safety

Kitchen safety doesn't stop at the microwave. What follows are pointers for avoiding other kitchen calamities:

◆ Wipe up any spills quickly. Water, and especially oil, can be slippery.

◆ If your youngster breaks a glass or a ceramic dish, have him cover it with a towel until you're able to clean it up. It's advisable to wear shoes in the kitchen for this reason.

◆ Keep electrical appliances away from water. Observe the manufacturers' safety guidelines about nonimmersible appliances such as coffee makers, electric-skillet control units, and waffle irons. Make sure hands are dry when touching electrical appliances.

◆ Follow manufacturers' rules when using pressure cookers, food processors, blenders, and mixers. Never try to defeat built-in safeguards.

◆ Teach your child to keep his hands out of the garbage disposal. The same goes for similar appliances, such as blenders and food processors.

◆ Observe your child using appliances and provide safety tips. If, for instance, your youngster uses an electric mixer, make sure he can control it and that he keeps rubber scrapers and other such utensils away from the beaters.

◆ Observe safety guidelines for storage and use of potentially toxic cleaning agents. (More details on this in 2, Store and Use Cleaning Supplies Safely.)

Practice Safety in the Bathroom

According to the National Safety Council, about 3 percent of all accidental deaths occurring at home take place in the bathroom. An estimated 150,000 nonfatal accidents occur there annually. Indeed there's great potential for trouble—trouble that can be avoided easily enough. The following guidelines will help keep your child safe in the bathroom—one of the most dangerous rooms in the house!

Toilet, Tub, and Shower

According to the National Safe Kids Campaign, drowning is the third leading cause of death in children. Drownings and near-drownings usually occur when children accidentally fall into pools or are left alone in the bathtub. You'll find pool safety in 7, Practice Swimming Pool Safety. Here, we'll tackle the problem of bathroom safety.

◆ Preschoolers can fall headfirst into toilets and drown. Keep the toilet lid down and the bathroom door closed. You might also consider installing a toilet seat lock.

◆ Bathtubs and showers are slippery. Use skid-proof strips or rubber, suction cup–backed bath mats to prevent falls on these hard surfaces.

◆ Don't leave bars of soap on the tub ledge. They can slip in, and your child can step on them and fall, possibly even drown. Instead, keep soap (even small pieces) in wall-mounted soap dishes.

◆ Install a handle in the bathtub stall. Make sure it is properly anchored with long screws into a wall beam (not just tile or plaster). With an L-shaped bar, your youngster can grab hold while sitting, standing, entering, and exiting the tub.

◆ Always supervise your kids in the tub. Children under the age of four can drown in as little as one inch of water. It only takes a minute or two. Never leave your youngster unattended in the bath—not even with an older sibling. If the phone is ringing, let it ring or take your child with you to answer it! Keep towels within arm's reach.

◆ To prevent scalding:
  ◆ Lower your water heater to "low," "warm," or 120°F. If you live in an apartment and your landlord is unwilling or unable to change the water temperature, install a cut-off device on your tub faucet and shower head that will shut down the water flow when it reaches 120°F.
  ◆ You can test the water's temperature by running the hot water for three to five minutes. Dip a hot water gauge or a mercury or liquid-crystal thermometer into the tub.
  ◆ Faucets that blend hot and cold water are the safest.
  ◆ Always test the water's temperature before putting your youngster in the tub. Dip your arm in past the elbow, since the temperature varies with depth. Keep in mind that your youngster's skin is more sensitive than yours.
  ◆ Don't allow your child to turn on the hot water without you. Again, be sure to supervise.

◆ Keep breakable glass bottles and jars (shampoo, conditioner, and so forth) out of the tub and shower area. If these fall on hard surfaces, they can shatter and cause injury. Recyclable plastic containers make better sense.

◆ Learn CPR and rescue breathing. What you learn can save a life during an emergency.

The Medicine Cabinet

Medicine cabinets can be lethal to young children. According to the National Safety Council, pain relievers are the fourth highest cause of poisoning among children under age six. Make sure that you purchase only over-the-counter products that come in childproof packaging. Here are some other precautions you can take:

◆ Ask your druggist for medications in childproof packages.

◆ Keep constant tabs on your preschooler's activities. When she gets too quiet, it's wise to suspect some potentially dangerous explorations are going on.

◆ Children are apt to climb and experiment. Keep all medications in an out-of-reach, locked compartment in your medicine cabinet. If you can't do this, find a different storage area that you can lock.

◆ Remember that laxatives, antacid "mints," mouthwash, and rubbing alcohol are also harmful if taken in large quantities. Store these like you would prescription medicine, and never refer to any medicine as "candy."

◆ Dispose of old or surplus prescription and nonprescription medications properly. Flush pills down the toilet and throw away their containers. Liquid medications should be washed down the drain. Rinse their bottles before disposing of them.

◆ Never give your youngster medicine in the dark. You may confuse his prescription with something else.

◆ It's wise to keep your child's medicine on a separate shelf from other family members'. You'll never confuse medications that way.

◆ Keep all medications in their original containers. Never switch medicines from one bottle to another, as this will only cause confusion.

◆ Keep cologne, aftershave, and other cosmetics out of children's reach.

◆ When visiting friends or relatives, ask that they remove potentially dangerous products and medications from your child's reach.

◆ In case of accidental poisoning, call your local poison control center. (See 1, Know How to Deal with Poisons.)

Electrical Appliances

The safe use of electrical appliances in the bathroom has been covered in 10, Check Electrical Appliances. But it bears repeating that you can avoid accidental electrocution by keeping all electrical appliances out of the bathroom. That includes radios, hair dryers, and free-standing electrical heaters. (Built-in heaters must be in good repair.)

If you have to use such electrical appliances as shavers or tooth-brushes, make sure they are battery driven or, at the very least, they're unplugged when not in use. Put them where they can't fall into a sinkful or a tubful of water. Teach your youngsters never to touch electrical appliances or even light switches either when their hands or bodies are wet or when they're standing in a water puddle.

Appliances that have the UL seal are the safest.

General Bathroom Safety

Other bathroom safety tips:

- Keep razors and razor blades locked in childproof cabinets. Dispose of them carefully, making sure your kids won't find them when rummaging in the trash.
- Store all cleaning products in high, childproof cabinets. (See 2, Store and Use Cleaning Supplies Safely for more specifics.) Never mix products containing chlorine bleach with those that contain ammonia, since this can create a poisonous gas.
- Glass or porcelain toothbrush holders and cups can shatter. Until your child is old enough to handle delicate *objets d'art,* stick to plastics, paper, and other such sturdy materials.
- Make sure if you're hanging hosiery or clothes up to dry in the bathroom that they don't drip on the floor where a child might slip and fall. Try using a plastic hanger hooked over the shower-head or a retractable clothes line strung over the tub.
- Use a night light.
- Be sure to close medicine-cabinet doors. Aside from inviting your curious child to explore, open cabinet doors have sharp corners that can cause nasty injuries.
- Make sure the bathroom door does not have a dead bolt or latch hook that would make entry nearly impossible from the outside. While you might value privacy, a door that won't open could prove fatal to an injured person locked within. Most modern locks have outside releases. Consider replacing older knobs and locks with such an assemblage.
- Hooks for towels and bathrobes should be hung above your head

to avoid eye or head injuries.

◆ If your hot water heater is in the bathroom, observe caution when using flammable substances such as nail polish, polish remover, alcohol, or aerosol deodorant and hairspray. It's wise to read product labels for precautions and to use these products in well-ventilated areas away from open flame.

Practice Safety in the Garage

The garage offers a plethora of potentially hazardous situations and products:

- Insecticides, rat poison, and snail bait
- Arts and crafts supplies such as linseed oil
- Rusty nails, junk, or other debris
- Liquid or granular fertilizers
- Motor oil, coolant, and antifreeze
- Power tools
- Turpentine, paint, and paint thinner and remover
- Hammers, vises, pliers, wrenches, and other pinch-evoking tools
- Charcoal lighter fluid
- Nails, awls, rasp files, handsaws, screwdrivers, and other sharp objects
- Shears, rakes, hedge and edge trimmers, lawn mowers, and other garden tools
- Gasoline and kerosene
- Oily or paint-covered rags

Did you know that as little as one teaspoon of antifreeze can kill an adult? Many of the products we store in the garage are highly flammable, highly toxic, or both.

If your garage looks like most—cluttered—your safest bet is to ban your kids from the area altogether. It's far from being an ideal playroom. Of course, total quarantine may be impossible, since you may need to store bikes or other play equipment there or you may enter the house directly through the garage. If your child must have access, teach him what is off limits. Explain the possible consequences to him (poisoning, severe injury, and so on.) if he doesn't abide by the precautions. And supervise, supervise, supervise.

What You Can Do

There are ways, however, to make your garage safer.

◆ Make sure all products come in childproof containers.

◆ Read and follow all safety precautions listed on label.

◆ Never store a product in anything but its original container.

◆ Never store flammable liquids in breakable glass containers. Keep small quantities in metal safety cans stored in locked cabinets on shelves that are too high for your child to reach, even if he stands on a chair. Be sure to use cabinets that are away from heat to store such liquids.

◆ Never use flammable liquids around open flames—even gas dryer, furnace, or water heater pilot lights.

◆ Store gasoline in a well-ventilated area in safety containers approved by Underwriters Laboratories.

◆ Store all poisonous products (fertilizers, rat poison, insecticides, motor oil) in hard-to-get-to locked closets. Out of sight, out of mind.

◆ Unplug and put away all electrical tools that are not in use.

◆ Stow your other tools in order and out of reach in childproof cabinets.

◆ Store garden tools in a shed or in a closed closet in your garage.

◆ Clean your garage regularly. Get rid of rusted or corroded containers and old magazines, newspapers, or clothes that can feed a fire.

◆ Store oily rags in closed metal cans.

◆ Keep a fire extinguisher in the garage.

If you're going to spend money childproofing your garage, your best investment may be in a professional childproofing service as well as a company that designs cabinets and closets. Some diaper companies even do childproofing on the side.

Call your local poison control center if your child has touched or swallowed poison. (Also refer to 1, Know How to Deal with Poisons, and Part VI, Fire Awareness.)

Test for and Deal with Asbestos

Asbestos is a fibrous material found in rocks that can resist fire or natural erosion. Because it's so durable, it has been used for many years to strengthen and insulate building materials. Microscopic airborne asbestos fibers can lodge in the lungs or be swallowed. Because they don't break down, these particles remain in the organs for a lifetime. Buildup from repeated exposure can cause *asbestosis,* a scarring and thickening within the alveoli, the tiny air sacs in the lungs. Over time that interferes with breathing and can cause heart failure. In addition, asbestos can cause lung cancer and *mesothelioma,* a cancer of the respiratory and digestive linings. (Smoking greatly enhances asbestos's cancer-causing properties.) Health effects may not appear until 15 to 40 years after exposure.

Because of these dangers, most products manufactured today do not contain asbestos. However, you might find asbestos:

- In insulating around hot water and steam pipes, boilers, and furnace ducts in homes built between 1920 and 1972.
- Within vinyl asbestos floor tiles, vinyl sheet flooring or adhesives sold before 1977.
- In wall and ceiling insulation in homes built between 1930 and 1950 and in insulating materials around wood burning stoves.
- As soundproofing or decorative materials sprayed on walls or ceilings, usually in homes built between 1945 and 1978.

◆ In patching, joint compounds, and textured paints
  applied before 1977.
◆ In asbestos cement roofing, shingles, and siding.
◆ In artificial logs, ashes, and embers used in fireplaces.
◆ In older housewares and home appliances such as:
  Hair dryers manufactured before 1979.
  Stove burner hot pads.
  Ironing board covers.
  Pot holders and oven mitts.

What You Should Do

According to the American Lung Association, the Consumer Product Safety Commission, and the EPA, the mere presence of asbestos in the home does not in itself constitute a safety hazard. In fact, these organizations stress that if the asbestos-containing material is in good condition and you're not planning to remodel your home, *it's best simply to leave it alone.* There is no danger if fibers are not released or inhaled. On the other hand, *improperly handled and removed asbestos can create a safety hazard for you and your family.*

Asbestos is usually bonded to other materials with strong bonding agents, which reduces the chance of fibers becoming airborne. Under the following circumstances, however, you might consider having a professional asbestos inspector and a trained, licensed asbestos contractor evaluate, repair, or remove this material from your home if:

◆ The asbestos shows signs of wear: tears, abrasions, or
  water damage.
◆ The asbestos is crumbling.
◆ You are disturbing or removing something that contains
  asbestos.
◆ Metal heating ducts insulated by asbestos have rusted
  through, exposing the asbestos to a constant flow of
  rushing, hot air that can make it airborne.
◆ You will be undertaking a remodeling project that calls
  for disturbing existing asbestos.

If you suspect that the asbestos in your home is releasing fibers, do not touch or remove the materials yourself. Instead, contact the American Industrial Hygiene Association or the EPA (the Resource Guide has the necessary information to do so.) for the names of labs that analyze asbestos using a technique called Polarized Light Microscopy. A professional asbestos inspector will collect samples to send to the lab and will provide a written evaluation of the extent of the problem as well as recommendations for corrective or preventive measures.

If, after careful consideration, you feel that the asbestos must be removed from your home, be sure to hire a licensed, state-certified asbestos contractor who has been trained by the EPA. The contractor and his employees should be thoroughly trained regarding asbestos hazards, appropriate work practices, and the use of personal protection devices. They should take the following precautions:

- ◆ The work area should be sealed off with plastic sheeting and duct tape and marked as a hazardous area. Workers should take great care not to track asbestos dust into the rest of your home. Heating and air conditioning systems should be shut down.
- ◆ Workers should wear approved respirators as well as protective gloves, hats, and other such clothing. These should be disposed of in sealed plastic bags after use.
- ◆ Asbestos should be sprayed with a fine mist of water and detergent (a teaspoon of detergent to a quart of water) to reduce the possibility of floating fibers.
- ◆ Workers should avoid breaking the asbestos into smaller pieces because that can release more fibers into the air.
- ◆ After being removed from your home, asbestos should be considered toxic waste and properly disposed of as such. Call the EPA or your local health department for advice. (See the Resource Guide.)
- ◆ Cleanup should include wet mopping. Dispose of mop heads and rags with the asbestos and contaminated clothing.
- ◆ Never dust, sweep, or vacuum suspected asbestos. Make sure your contractor uses a specialized HEPA (high-efficiency particulate air) vacuum cleaner.

Other Precautions You Can Take

◆ Don't allow children or pets into the asbestos removal area.

◆ Don't allow children to play in dusty areas around asbestos-insulated furnaces or ducts.

◆ When replacing asbestos vinyl flooring, it's best to cover the old floor rather than to sand, scrape, or otherwise damage materials that contain asbestos.

Teach Your Child Gun Safety

ccording to a June 1987 article in the *Journal of the American Medical Association,* firearms rank among the top 10 causes of death in our nation. They account for at least 30,000 deaths per year, with accidental gun-related fatalities being the most common among children. Boys are nearly nine times more likely than girls to die from unintentional gunshot wounds, probably because of the male fascination with firearms. Most self-inflicted wounds occur at home, in the room in which the unlocked, loaded gun is stored. Experts have found that unintentional fatal shootings of friends or family in the home is 6 to 12 times more common than fatal shootings of criminals. (In the state of Washington, for example, only two of the 398 gun-related in-home deaths between 1978 and 1983 were of intruders.)

Let's face it: Guns are agents of death and destruction. As one expert put it, "Firearms are designed to be used by conscripted soldiers, and an unspoken criterion of their design is that they be operable even by an idiot under stress. A halfway intelligent child, given time at their leisure to play with one, will eventually figure out how to bypass any safety mechanism, load, and shoot the gun." *You cannot childproof a gun, but you can gunproof your child.*

The Police Executive Research Forum, a Washington, D.C., group of police chiefs and criminal-justice experts, recommends the following precautions:

- ◆ If you own a gun, never leave it loaded. (If you've loaded it, say, in the event of an emergency, remember to unload it once the danger has passed.)

- Keep your gun under lock and key and carry the key on you. (If you hide a gun under your pillow while you sleep, never leave it—not even for a minute or two—unattended.)
- Lock up your ammunition separate from your gun.
- Ask the parents of your child's friends if they own guns. If so, insist that they observe the above precautions. (If not, I wouldn't allow my youngster to play in their homes.)
- Make sure the gun's safety catch functions properly.

It's imperative that you impress upon your child the dangers of playing with real guns. Be sure he knows not to touch a firearm without your supervision. That means that if a playmate's parents own a gun, your youngster is not to touch it.

Darlene Duffy Darling's 10-year-old, Brian, was accidentally killed by a friend playing with his parents' gun. Her advice to parents, which appeared in the May 1989 *Ladies' Home Journal,* is that they tell their children that "if they do come across a gun at a friend's house or anyplace else, to leave the room immediately and notify an adult that the gun is out." The Darling family has produced an instructional gun-safety videotape, *Brian's Message,* which you may find helpful. (See the Resource Guide for more details.)

PART II

On the Road

Understand Street Hazards and Teach Traffic Rules

When I was a child, my mother used to sing to me:

Let the ball roll
Let the ball roll
No matter where it may go...

and:

When you ride your bicycle,
Look out for the motor cars.
When you ride your bicycle,
Keep your hands on the handlebars.

Although the rest of the verses have since faded from memory, their meaning has not. The street presents myriad hazards to children. Indeed, close encounters between child and car can inflict severe, sometimes fatal, injury. In fact, a pedestrian hit by a car is 220 times more likely to die as a result than either a passenger or driver who has collided with another car.

There are about 150,000 pedestrian-car accidents a year, according to the National Safety Council. Of those, nearly 50 percent involve children 14 or younger. Kids between ages five and nine suffer the greatest risk because they are more likely to dart out into the street without looking, and boys are twice as likely as girls to be involved in accidents since boys often play in the street.

To keep your child safe, you must understand which situations pose a danger, supervise your youngster carefully if he's near traffic, and teach him the rules of the road.

Why Kids Have Traffic Troubles

According to the National Safety Council, the preponderance of car-pedestrian accidents occur in the afternoon and early evening—when kids are on the street and when visibility is poor. Children below the age of nine seem to have more accidents during the spring and summer months, probably because they're out playing more.

Many playtime activities can create street hazards for your child:
- Darting between two parked cars into traffic.
- Riding his Big Wheel, tricycle, or wagon across the street. These low-to-the-ground toys are difficult for drivers to see.
- Dashing across the street in order to intercept a passing ice cream truck.
- Chasing a ball into the street.
- Walking behind the school bus or running into traffic to catch the bus.

Moreover, according to the Safe Kids Campaign, children under age eight have many misconceptions about traffic:
- They believe that if they can see the driver, the driver can see them, too.
- They think cars stop instantaneously.
- Very young children may see cars as affable, living beings. (That misconception may be reinforced by cartoon-character cars, as seen in such movies as *Who Framed Roger Rabbit?* as well as in TV commercials.)

Besides these errors, young children may not recognize or react quickly to danger. They may have a hard time determining where a sound (such as a honking horn) comes from. They may have difficulty judging the speed of a car. Finally, their field of vision is considerably smaller than an adult's.

Supervise Your Child

The best way to teach children street safety is to spend time with them on the street. Hold your young child's hand when in the street and in parking lots. Cross the street with him (explaining the safest way to do it) many hundreds of times before you allow him to do it himself at about age seven or eight. He should ask your permission to cross the street, and you should witness his first several dozen crossings, just to be sure he follows the rules you've taught him.

Establish appropriate consequences if your youngster goes into the street without stopping, looking, and listening. For example, you can say, "You didn't follow the safety rules. You won't be able to play in the front yard till next Monday. That's when I'll give you another chance to show me that you understand the rules and can follow them." Be sure to follow up consistently. As my grandmother used to say, "It's better for him to cry over lost privileges than for you to cry."

If your kindergartener or first-grader will be walking to school, walk the route with him many times during the summer. In my opinion, kids aren't ready to walk to school on their own till they're about eight years old, but daily practice will help your youngster internalize the rules you've taught. That way, he'll be ready, and you'll feel more at ease, when the school year comes.

Most important, be a good role model. After you've instructed your child to cross only at intersections and only with green lights, don't confuse him with contradictory acts. Children are more apt to mimic what we do than what we say.

Teach Your Child Traffic Rules

Once you recognize the potential hazards, you can teach your youngster how to avoid them. Have her follow these rules:

◆ Only cross at the street corner or at a marked crosswalk, and never in the middle of the street.
◆ Never run into the street, especially between parked cars.
◆ Never chase a ball into the street. Let it roll till it stops, and call an adult to recover it.
◆ Never chase a pet into the street. Call an adult.
◆ Never play in the street or drive your Big Wheel or tricycle into the street without an adult there.
◆ Never assume the car driver can see you.
◆ If you're not sure a street is safe to cross, ask me.
◆ Follow the **stop, look,** and **listen** rule: Before crossing the street,

stop at the curb. **Look** to the left, the right, and then back to the left again. **Listen** for traffic. (If your child is too young to tell left from right, tell her to look "this way" and "that way" and then "this way again.")

♦ Wait until it's safe, meaning there are no cars coming in either direction, before crossing.

♦ Keep looking both ways as you cross.

♦ Walk only on the sidewalks. If there are no sidewalks, walk to the left, facing traffic.

♦ Cross only with a "Walk" sign or a green light, never with a flashing "Don't Walk" or a yellow light.

♦ Watch for cars that may be turning right on a red light.

♦ If the street is too wide to cross in one light, wait at the safety island in the middle of the road. Be sure to stand on the elevated area, not in the street.

♦ Stand on the curb, never in the street, while waiting for lights to change.

♦ Wear light-colored, white, or reflective clothing when walking at night. (If you live in a rural area, it might be wise to carry a flashlight, too.)

♦ Follow the directions of policemen and traffic guards.

♦ Walk directly across the street. Don't stop or dawdle.

♦ Never cross a street diagonally unless traffic lights are coordinated so that all traffic stops at once.

♦ Always get out of the car on the curb side, never on the traffic side.

Keep in mind that most car-pedestrian accidents occur in residential areas, close to home.

Buckle Up for Safety

Recently, I witnessed a scene that turned my stomach. A well-dressed, obviously well-off couple in a fancy European sedan was talking with their young son, who stood behind them, between their seats, on the car floor. These parents may have "made it" in the world, but they sure haven't made it in my book. As I drove behind them, I kept wondering, why haven't these folks buckled that kid up? Forget about the fact that seatbelt fastening is required by law in my state; didn't they understand that they were exposing their child to potentially great bodily harm? Didn't they care about him?

I suppose, like many people, this couple believed that seatbelts are unnecessary. Indeed, according to a recent study by the U.S. Department of Health and Human Services, about 42 percent of all American children—more than 17 million—don't usually buckle up. Parents may ascribe to the myths that children are safest when held in their arms or that a seatbelt will entrap the child during a fiery crash or a plunge into a river. Perhaps this couple believes that they can grab their child during an accident or that being thrown free of a crash is safer than sitting through one. Or maybe this couple just didn't want to suffer through yet another tantrum as their preschooler resisted being restrained.

Whatever the reason, failure to buckle up a child or to teach him to use his seatbelt is highly irresponsible. Your child is simply not safe in your lap. During an accident, the force of impact may tear her from your arms or cause you to crush her against the dashboard with your own weight. Even if the car were to become engulfed in flames or submerged in water (relatively rare occurrences), seatbelts would protect her from injury at the time of impact, so she would be better able to flee to safety.

Moreover, it's nearly impossible to grab a child during an accident. Collisions usually happen so quickly, parents have no time to react. And being thrown clear of the car is no picnic either. According to the National Safe Kids Campaign, your chances of dying in a car accident are 25 times greater if you're thrown from the vehicle. As this organization so aptly put it, "Think about it—[if you're not buckled up] there are only two ways out—through an open door or through the glass."

How to Buckle Up Your Child Properly

If your youngster is under 40 pounds or under the age of four, you'll still need to use a safety seat. Follow the manufacturer's installation instructions to the letter. Here are some additional precautions you should take with your child's safety seat:

- Make sure the seatbelt is threaded through the proper slots on the seat.
- The harness and seatbelt should be tight.
- Make sure to fasten the harness. Without it, your child is vulnerable to being thrown free.
- If you're flying to a destination where you'll be renting a car, check your child's car seat with your other baggage.
- If you rent a car while your own is being repaired, take your child's car seat along for the ride.

If your youngster has outgrown the safety seat, it's time to graduate to a safety belt. Some tips on proper belt use:

- Fasten the belt low and tight against your child's hips. The belt shouldn't squeeze the abdomen.
- If the shoulder strap of the belt presses on your child's throat or face, put it behind her. Until she's taller, you'll have to rely solely on the lap belt.
- Never place the shoulder belt under your child's arm, where it could break her ribs during an accident.
- If your child is large enough for a shoulder strap, make

sure it's snug and in proper working order. It should
lock when tugged sharply.

◆ If your child somehow resists the seatbelt, be firm in
your resolve to buckle her up. Her life depends on it.

◆ Never disconnect your car's seatbelt warning beeper.
Although it may seem annoying, remember: It's there to
protect you and your family.

◆ Never drive your car—even for a short errand—without
buckling up yourself. You teach by example.

◆ Instruct your child to buckle up no matter what,
whether in relatives' or friends' cars or in a carpool. The
ritual should become automatic.

Everyone always needs to buckle up—even for short hops.
Remember, most car accidents occur close to home; you drive
around your neighborhood more than anywhere else!

Insist on Bicycle Safety

The Consumer Product Safety Commission estimates that 1 million injury-causing bicycle accidents occur each year. Many of these mishaps could be prevented by teaching children to take proper precautions.

Wear That Helmet

Bike helmets are not pretty things, and kids can really resist wearing them. They do, however, protect against dangerous head injuries that can cause permanent disablement and death. According to the National Safety Council, more than three out of four bicycle-related fatalities or permanent disabilities result from head injuries.

Helmets should be a nonnegotiable aspect of the bike-riding experience. You might acquaint your youngster with wearing protective headgear early on when you take him out for a ride in his kiddie seat. You can also point out to a balky youngster that his favorite football player wears a helmet. Make sure your child wears his each and every time he goes out for a ride.

Purchase helmets that are intended exclusively for cycling. Helmets that have been awarded a Snell or ANSI seal of approval have passed rigorous safety tests and are the only ones you should consider. Also, no matter what color the helmet, make sure your child's has reflective material on it for higher visibility during night riding. Since vented helmets permit air circulation, they may be more comfortable.

The helmet must fit correctly in order for it to properly absorb impact. Helmets manufactured for children are adjustable and can "grow" with your youngster. A helmet that is too loose will slide around or pull off with the chin strap still fastened. It shouldn't slip forward or slide far back on the head but should sit comfortably right on the crown, slightly over the forehead. Ask the salesperson at a bicycle shop to advise you about the proper fit. The strap must be buckled, of course, in order to prevent the headgear from flying off during a spill. Warn your youngster not to trade helmets with a friend: The other child's head may be a different size and the helmet may not fit well.

Choose a Bike That Fits

Many parents buy bicycles too large for their youngsters in the mistaken belief that their kids will "grow into" the vehicle. The fact is, kids who are too small for their bikes have a harder time learning to ride because they have more difficulty controlling it. Buying a bicycle that's too big places your child at risk for accidents and injury, and that's no fun for him! Besides, properly fitted bikes will last for years with timely seat and handlebar adjustments: The 16-inch bike—with high-rise handlebars—you purchase for your seven-year-old can last until he turns 11. By preadolescence, he'll be tall enough for a 24- or 26-inch bicycle.

I strongly recommend purchasing your child's bike at a bicycle shop rather than a toy, general sporting goods, or department store. Although bicycle shops may cost a little more, you must also factor in that you are paying for expert service and advice. Salespeople in bicycle shops are often avid cyclers themselves and are quite knowledgeable about correct frame size, helmet fit, and so on.

To test for proper fit, ask your youngster to sit on the seat and push one pedal to its lowest position. If the seat is at the right height, your child's foot will be comfortably parallel to the ground. He should also easily straddle a men's bicycle frame while standing. The seat should be parallel to the ground, and his torso should lean forward slightly when he holds the handlebars. High-rise handlebars should never be higher than shoulder level, or your child may not have enough control.

Instill a Healthy Respect for Traffic

Bicycles are vehicles, not toys. Once your child is old enough to take his bike into the street (at about age nine), he will have all the legal rights and responsibilities of any driver. It is therefore vital for him to learn bike safety rules. A class at the local YMCA or a bicycling badge in the Scouts will help teach him what he needs to know. It's also important for you to properly maintain the bike. Have trained bicycle mechanics make major adjustments and repairs.

Bicycle Safety Rules

Bicycle safety is based on your youngster's ability to control his vehicle, his visibility to other drivers, and the predictability of his behavior. Teach your child the following rules:

- Until age nine, he should ride only on sidewalks, park bike paths, patios, and other places away from traffic.
- Once your youngster demonstrates to you that he is responsible enough to ride the streets, teach him to **stop, look** (both ways), and **listen** before he exits a driveway onto the street. He should wait for traffic to pass. (It might boost his confidence and your peace of mind if you accompany him on his first few bike rides in traffic.)
- Your cyclist should ride with the direction of traffic on the right side of the street. (This is the opposite of pedestrian rules.) But he should also give himself enough room to avoid such hazards as a driver opening his car door.
- He must obey all traffic signs and signals, such as letting cars pass at stop signs and slowing down at yield signs.
- He should look for traffic behind and in front when making a right or left turn.
- It's recommended that children under age 12 walk their bikes across intersections.
- He must learn and use proper hand signals to warn motorists of his intentions. (Left arm at a right angle up means right turn; left arm at a right angle down means stop; left hand straight out means left turn.)
- He must never ride a friend on the handlebars or crossbar.
- He should avoid listening to headphones. Loud music is distract-

ing and can drown out important traffic noises like approaching vehicles, sirens, and honking horns.

◆ He should avoid riding in the dark until he's at least 12 years old. (If he stays at a friend's house until after dark, he should call you for a ride home.)

◆ You are the best role model. Follow bike safety rules yourself, and your job as teacher will be much easier.

Safety Equipment

Since your child's safety depends on his visibility to other drivers, it's important to equip his bike with accessories that will make him more obvious. These include:

◆ Headlights: The lamp should throw light 500 feet. It should be used for night riding and during adverse conditions such as rain, fog, and so forth.

◆ Reflectors: Federal law requires that bicycles sold in the U.S. have red rear reflectors that are visible from 600 feet. The bike should also have clear or yellow pedal reflectors and side reflectors on rims or tires.

◆ Taillights: Though not required, these increase visibility.

◆ Flags: Bikes equipped with flags on five-foot flexible rods are more visible.

◆ Bells, horns, whistles: These warn pedestrians that a bike is approaching.

Other safety equipment you should consider:

◆ A carrying rack on the rear ensures that your child will not be distracted by lugging packages or books.

◆ Clips that gather loose pant legs prevent fabric from tangling in the chain or spokes.

Kiddie Seats

If your preschooler still rides behind you in a kiddie seat, make sure the seat has a high back for support and padding for comfort. It should also have a seat belt and leg shields to protect your child's legs from the spokes. Attach the kiddie seat to the rear frame of your bike for greatest stability.

Avoid Skate and
Skateboard Accidents

O ne of the worst roller-skating mishaps in my family occurred when my daughter was skating in the house. No, she didn't fall on the slick floors. She rolled over my bare toes! You can rest assured that she never skated in the house again.

As with bicycles, the distinction between plaything and vehicle blurs when it comes to roller skates, in-line skates (such as Rollerblades), and skateboards. I recommend riding these wheeled toys only on the sidewalk. When your child rides in the street, she becomes part of traffic—and that's not the safest place to be, especially since she has less control than if she were walking! Hitching a ride on a moving vehicle—even a bicycle—is extremely dangerous and to be avoided.

Your child must choose sidewalks wisely. She should avoid those with deep ruts, cracks, or tree roots pushing the concrete up at crazy angles. And she should be especially careful if she lives or plays in a hilly community. While some youngsters may enjoy the thrill of speed, greater speed means more serious injuries, should they take a spill. If you live in such a neighborhood, a trip to a skating rink or a park with paved walkways in a flatter part of town is advisable.

Jumping, "popping wheelies," and skateboarding off ramps and curbs are also dangerous practices. Regrettably, boys often get caught up in competitive, macho games in which they attempt to outdo one another at these activities. As I can attest from firsthand experience (watching the consequences of a neighbor's son's stunts), bones are easily broken and crushed during such contests. Children under the age of eight are too young for skateboards.

Ice skating should only take place at rinks or ponds that your community's authorities have designated as safe. Teach your child to observe and obey "Thin Ice" signs. Your youngster should never ice skate in the street (unless it has been roped off for that purpose) or wear her ice skates to or from ice rinks, even with protective guards on the blades.

Children using roller skates, ice skates, and skateboards should wear protective gear: helmets and elbow and knee pads or guards. Although roller skaters and skateboarders may cross quiet streets when the traffic has cleared (see 18, Understand Street Hazards and Teach Traffic Rules), it's inadvisable for them to cross busy intersections in skates or on their boards until they're 11 or 12. It's hard enough getting the hang of it on foot!

In the World

Teach Your Child the Basics

As soon as your youngster is old enough to talk or sing along with a nursery rhyme, you should begin teaching her her name, parents' names, address (including city), and phone number with area code. If she becomes lost or abducted, or is involved in any other emergency situation, she'll be able to provide this useful information to the police. To help your child along, you might put your phone number to a nursery rhyme like "Twinkle Twinkle Little Star" or "Rock-a-Bye Baby."

It's also imperative that she knows how to contact law enforcement and emergency personnel. The Los Angeles Police Department advises that you teach your child to dial 9-1-1. Some children interpret these numbers to mean 9-11. Of course, there's no 11 on the phone button pad or dial, so in an emergency these kids may become confused and fail to reach the help they need. It's best to practice with your preschooler on a play phone until she understands the procedure.

If your community is not served by 9-1-1, instruct your child to dial 0 for Operator in order to reach help. Your youngster should give the operator all the information he requests.

With either form of emergency phone service, it's crucial that your youngster stay on the line (unless, of course, a fire is smoking her out of the house) so that the operator can get all the relevant information. In the worst case, if your child doesn't provide an address or phone number, the call can be traced through an open phone line.

A new telephone device called Phone Home can help your child make emergency phone calls. The gadget—smaller than a deck of cards—can be programmed with your home number. In order to call home, your youngster would position the device over the mouthpiece and push a button labeled "home." Phone Home can also connect your child to an operator or 9-1-1 emergency service. It costs about $20 and can be obtained by calling (800) 447-5196. In independent testing, 3- to 12-year-olds used Phone Home with little difficulty. The device has been endorsed by the Vanished Children's Alliance, based in San Jose, California, and the Missing Children Division of the National Child Safety Council in Washington, D.C.

It's also wise for any child who is old enough to play on the sidewalk or cross the street by herself to carry some form of identification. Should she become hurt, emergency personnel would be unable to reach you without it.

Document Your Child's Identity

While parents need not be fearful about the possibility of kidnapping, they should be cautious. Such is the wisdom of the National Center for Missing and Exploited Children. The center suggests five steps you can take to prepare for the "remote possibility" that your youngster is abducted.

1. Keep a complete description of your child. Write down your child's height, weight, hair and eye color, and date of birth. Include identifying markers such as unusual birthmarks, glasses or lenses, braces, scars, pierced earrings, and so on.

2. Take a color photo of your child every six months. Make sure the picture is clear and accurately portrays how your child looks—a picture of him in a Halloween costume and face paint won't do. Head shots taken from different angles are best.

3. Ask your dentist to prepare dental charts of your child. These should be updated every time your child's teeth are examined or worked on. The charts should include written records and current X-rays. If you move, be sure to take the dental records with you until you find a new dentist.

4. Keep track of your child's medical records. Police use medical records, especially X-rays, to help identify children who have been recovered. Make sure that all permanent scars, broken bones, birthmarks, and blemishes have been recorded. Ask your physician where your child's records are located and how you can obtain copies if need be.

5. Fingerprint your child. Fingerprints must be taken properly in order for the police to be able to use them. Most police departments and communities provide fingerprinting services. Be sure to keep your copy of the fingerprints and photos in a safe place; the police do not keep copies of these.

Help Your Child Deal with Strangers

hen I was a child, my parents endlessly repeated "Never talk to strangers." To me, that meant I must keep my distance from the sweet old lady behind us in line at the grocery store as well as the wild-eyed vagrant hovering around the playground. I was properly chastened.

Experts in child abduction and exploitation point out, however, that most incidents involving kidnapping or sexual abuse are perpetrated by people who are familiar to the child but perhaps unfamiliar to the parents. A child's conception of the word *stranger*, therefore, may work to her disadvantage. For example, she may believe *stranger* means only someone she has never seen or spoken to before. Unfortunately, kidnappers and child abusers often befriend youngsters before trying to exploit them.

Indeed, the National Center for Missing and Exploited Children recommends that it's "more appropriate to teach our children to be on the lookout for certain kinds of *situations* or *actions* rather than certain kinds of individuals." Just because your child is acquainted with an individual doesn't make that person safe.

Actions and Situations
Your Child Should Be Aware Of

◆ Your youngster should be wary of any adult who asks for help. It's entirely appropriate for a child to need help from an adult, but an adult has no business asking a youngster to assist him—even if he's looking for a "lost kitten."

- Your youngster should avoid any unfamiliar adult who knows her name. Someone devious can easily ascertain a youngster's name by listening to conversations among playmates or by reading identifying inscriptions on backpacks and lunch boxes. For that reason, T-shirts with names emblazoned can invite disaster.
- Your youngster should steer clear of anyone following her in a car or van. (See 25, Prevent Kidnappings.)
- She should run from individuals offering to take her picture.
- She should avoid people offering her candy or toys.
- She should keep away from anyone asking her to keep a special secret or play a special game.

Teach your youngster that merely having seen or met a person before does not make him safe. Perhaps it's best to stress that she shouldn't talk to anyone she hasn't seen *with you*. Trustworthy adults usually include parents, teachers, close relatives and family friends, playmates' parents, friendly neighbors, clergy, policemen, and well-known merchants in the community.

What You Can Do to Help

The National Safety Council suggests that you role-play different situations with your youngster to help her prepare for an emergency. Depending on your child's age, you can use dolls or puppets to demonstrate the appropriate watchful, cautious behavior, or you can play the "stranger" yourself. Observe how your child responds to the situations you present, and gently teach her a safer approach if she seems too gullible or easily swayed.

Teach your child that she should report to you if she sees the same person hanging or sneaking around the park frequently, talking to little kids, or cruising the neighborhood in a car. If you live in an apartment building with an elevator, remind her that she need not get in the elevator if she feels suspicious of or uncomfortable with an occupant. She can wait for the next car or can take the stairs.

Prevent Kidnappings

Kidnapping is a frightful prospect, but you can teach your child to protect himself. First, he should follow the guidelines in 24, Help Your Child Deal with Strangers, regarding strangers. But there are other precautionary measures you can both take to prevent tragedy. Before you carry out the following safeguards, explain to your child why it's imperative to do so.

- Be sure you know where your child is at all times. If he must come home to an empty house, establish a routine in which he calls you at work or checks in with a trusted neighbor as soon as he walks in the house. (See 6, Teach Your Child Latchkey Safety.)
- Familiarize yourself with your child's daily activities and his friends and acquaintances. That way, you'll better know where he's apt to be and can reach him by phone if he's late returning home.
- Before your youngster visits a friend or goes to the mall, library, or park, he must check in with you. He should tell you where he's going, with whom, his mode of transportation, and when he'll return. He might even leave a phone number if he's going to a friend's home.
- If your child is late in coming home, insist that he call you for a ride rather than walking home alone in the dark.
- Insist that your child ask your permission before accepting a ride from anyone—even people he knows. He should also get your clearance to accept money, presents,

or candy.

◆ Have your youngster rely on the buddy system: It's best for him to be with a friend wherever he goes.

◆ He should avoid anyone who wants to talk to him from a car or van.

What Your Child Should Do
When Being Followed

If your child feels that he's being followed, the National Safety Council suggests several strategies he can take to elude his pursuer:

1. He should safely cross the street.

2. If a car is following him, he should reverse direction suddenly. The car will have to make a U-turn to continue the pursuit.

3. He should walk faster or run toward the nearest well-lit public area, such as a minimall or gas station.

4. He should wave or call to an imagined friend.

5. He should run into a store or your house, provided someone is home, or flag down a passing police car.

6. If nobody is home, he should go to a trusted neighbor's house and wait there till you return.

7. If he is caught, he should try to get loose and run home. If he can't get away, he should scream "Help," "Fire," "He's not my father," "She's trying to take me," or some other statement that will draw others' attention.

8. He should report any unusual situation to you. You may wish to file a police report.

9. If you're unavailable, he should dial 9-1-1 himself, or he should tell a neighbor what happened and have the neighbor call the police.

Teach Your Child What to Do If He Becomes Lost

What adult has not lived through the terrifying experience of becoming a "lost child"? And what more terrifying experience than to have a child who's lost? Whether at the beach or in a department store, it's easy for a youngster to suddenly become disoriented and lose you. He turns his back for a minute, and suddenly you're gone.

To help your youngster become "unlost" in these situations, teach him how to react beforehand. That will prevent him from panicking and running wild-eyed through the store, screaming for "Mommmmmeeee!"

When your child realizes he is lost, he should:

◆ Stop wandering around in search of you. He'll only get more lost and confused.

◆ Go to a checkout counter, security guard, lost and found, lifeguard, manager's office, or other official and say, "I lost my mommy and daddy."

◆ Wait with security personnel until you've been paged and located.

◆ As an extra precaution, be sure your child knows his name, his parents' names, his address (including the city), and phone number with area code.

Know What to Do If Your Child Is Missing

You must spring into action *immediately* if you believe your youngster is missing. The National Center for Missing and Exploited Children suggests that you take the following steps:

1. If your youngster is missing from home, search your house first. Go through every closet; look in your laundry basket, under beds, in the toy box, behind the garage, in the basement, or any other place your youngster might hide or become entrapped. Call neighbors and friends to ask if they've seen your child.

2. If your child is missing on an outing, contact security. If you're in a store, office building, park, or at the beach, notify the security office, store manager, ranger, or lifeguard.

3. Call the police. If you can't locate your youngster in the expected places, don't waste a moment. Stay calm so that you can communicate clearly. Give your name and location and say, *"Please send an officer. I want to report a missing child."*

Give the officer any identifying information you can, including a description of your child's height, weight, clothes, braces, pierced earrings, hair and eye color, and any scars or marks. Explain where and when you noticed your child was missing.

The police will respond quickly if your child is under 13, handicapped or needing daily medication, or if she may be the object of foul play.

4. Provide identifying documentation. If you have fingerprinted, photographed, or otherwise documented your child's identity, now is the time to share that information with the police. Offer what dental and medical records you can. (See 23, Document Your

Child's Identity.)

5. Cooperate with the police. You may be asked further questions or be given instructions. It's important to be helpful and follow directions.

6. Request that your child be entered immediately into the FBI's National Crime Information Center Missing Persons File. This national network will ensure that the police will be able to identify and return your child, should she turn up in any other community. The FBI can also enter this information or verify what's already been entered.

7. Call the National Center for Missing and Exploited Children (NCMEC). The center will take any information you have to offer. A case manager may work with you and the police department in locating your child. The center can also refer you to a support group in your community. NCMEC also arranges for pictures of missing youngsters to be displayed around the country. (See the Resource Guide for NCMEC's phone number.)

Prevent Sexual Abuse

Sexual abuse includes any interaction between a child and an individual older than him who uses the child for sexual gratification. Sexual abuse does not necessitate some form of penetration. It can also include fondling, masturbation, sexual innuendos, inappropriate kissing, voyeurism, exhibitionism, and pornography. Both boys and girls are victims of abuse.

In *The Right to Innocence* (Jeremy Tarcher, 1989), Los Angeles child sexual abuse specialist Beverly Engel explains that the abuser need not be an adult. Normal sexual exploration games between "consenting peers," such as two preschoolers playing doctor, occur "only between those of the same age, sexual experience, and power." But sexual activity between a preschooler and school-age child or adolescent constitutes sexual abuse.

Most abusive situations are not sudden and violent, as rape might be. Often, the child is coerced or duped into sexual activity over a period of time *by a person whom he knows*. The abuser may make misleading statements such as, "Let's play the game that I used to play when I was a kid," or, "You won't be my friend anymore if you don't do what I ask." Or the abuser may promise candy or other treats as an inducement.

What You Can Do

According to child abuse experts, the best way to prevent child abuse is to have an open, loving relationship with your youngster— one in which he can trust you with his innermost feelings. Children who feel neglected, abandoned, or unloved are more vulnerable to being abused since they may respond favorably to others' overtures in order to alleviate their loneliness.

In addition to cultivating a positive relationship with your child, it is your responsibility to teach him to protect himself. Be sure to communicate the following points to your youngster—not to frighten him, but to let him know that he has power and ought to be careful:

- ◆ Some touching is "good" and some is "bad." No one should touch him on the private parts of his body— those covered by underwear or a bathing suit.
- ◆ If someone touches him in a way that feels frightening or uncomfortable, or asks him to perform acts that evoke those same feelings, he must say "No!," then run away and tell his parents or another trusted adult.
- ◆ He should pay attention to and trust his feelings. If he feels frightened or uncomfortable about an incident, he should tell his parents right away.
- ◆ His family loves him and will listen if he has a problem that confuses or upsets him.
- ◆ He can and should come to his parents for help even if the incident was some time ago. It's never too late to seek help.
- ◆ If someone touches him in his private places, approaches him to keep a "special" secret, or threatens his loved ones if he doesn't keep quiet, he should tell his parents anyway.
- ◆ His body is special and private. He deserves respect and a sense of safety. He has the right to say no to anyone who is bothering him.
- ◆ He is not alone. No matter what happens to him, his parents will love him and stand by him.

It also behooves you to to take note of any adult or older child who hovers around your youngster or provides him with presents or treats. If your child's behavior changes suddenly and radically, sit down and have a heart-to-heart conversation with him about what's going on in his life. (See 29, Know How to Recognize and Respond to the Signs of Sexual Abuse.)

Know How to Recognize and Respond to the Signs of Sexual Abuse

One of the most painful thoughts for parents to bear is the suspicion that their child has been sexually abused. What should you look for if you fear that abuse has occurred? Childhelp USA and the National Center for Missing and Exploited Children—two organizations dedicated to fighting childhood sexual abuse—give the following guidelines. Take special note if:

◆ Your child's behavior changes dramatically—she withdraws, experiences severe mood swings, cries excessively, or acts frightened.

◆ Your child suddenly becomes angry, aggressive, or rebellious.

◆ Your child acts out inappropriate sexual behavior with dolls or other youngsters. She may show an unusual, seemingly adult interest in or knowledge of sexuality, or her behavior may imply sexual involvement with an adult or older child.

◆ Your child experiences sleep disturbances, such as bed-wetting, nightmares, or fear of going to sleep.

◆ Your child's behavior regresses, becoming more immature.

◆ Your child becomes inexplicably fearful of certain places or people. She may become frantic at being left alone with an abuser.

◆ Your child experiences itching, pain, bleeding, bruises, oozing of fluid, or chafing in the genital area.

◆ Your child has been diagnosed with a venereal disease or

is pregnant.
◆ Your child suddenly spends a great deal of time in her fantasy world.
◆ Your child seems to act seductively or, conversely, she fears intimate contact with others.

What Should You Do If You Suspect Abuse?

1. First and foremost, stay calm and don't blame or criticize your child. In cases of child abuse (sexual or otherwise), youngsters are *always* the victims. Tell your child that you will protect her from further contact with the perpetrator—and do so!

2. Take your youngster to your physician for confirmation and treatment. Often, children who have been sexually abused have also suffered physical trauma.

3. Report the abuse to the police and to an appropriate community agency such as the Department of Protective Services or the Department of Social Services. (You can locate these in your phone book. If you have trouble finding an agency, call Childhelp's national 24-hour hotline: (800) 4-A-CHILD.) Sexual abuse is illegal, and these agencies will conduct an investigation.

4. If your child has revealed the disturbing news of abuse, tell her that *you believe her and that you know she is not at fault.* Make it clear to your youngster that she is blameless and that the perpetrator is entirely at fault. Children often blame themselves for the abuse. Child-abuse experts emphasize that youngsters rarely make up stories of abuse. Any revelation may be a cry for help. Make sure you let your child know that you will stand by her with your love and support.

5. Respect your youngster's privacy. Don't share her story or discuss it in front of anyone who has no need to hear it.

6. Praise your child's courage in coming forth. Often, abusers and molesters silence children with threats of further violence—to pets, parents, or themselves. Moreover, your child might find the situation embarrassing and thus difficult to share. She may feel "dirty" and fear losing your love. You can say to your child something like, "I know telling me this is difficult for you, but I'm really glad you

did. You did the right thing. I'm going to help you deal with it."

7. Be affectionate and supportive. Express your heartfelt belief that she is a good person. Offer your love and encouragement by saying, "This wasn't your fault," or, "I'm sorry this happened to you, but together we'll get through it." Give lots of hugs and kisses if your child is open to receiving them.

8. Seek psychological counseling for your child. Any way you look at it, your youngster has suffered emotional and physical trauma, the scars of which can last a lifetime without proper treatment. It's imperative that *within six months of the incident* you seek out a child therapist who specializes or is experienced in the treatment of sexual abuse. Otherwise, coping strategies your child develops to deal with the assault, such as withdrawal or rebelliousness, may become a permanent part of her personality.

Local rape crisis clinics, social service agencies, and professional psychology or social work associations may be helpful in your search. With very young children, the therapist may rely on play therapy with dolls, sandbox, and puppets to help your youngster express her feelings and reexperience (and thus free herself of) the incident.

Teach Your Child How to Behave Around Others' Pets

Teach your youngster how to interact with friends' and neighbors' pets. Dogs and cats should be neither frightened nor teased. Cats will scratch and bite when provoked. Dogs will respond with equal hostility and may even attack. Loud noises, such as screaming, may also frighten a dog into an attack. Youngsters should keep away from dogs that fiercely protect their territory from "intruders." Bared teeth, growling, down-pointed tail, pulled-back ears, glowering eyes, and vociferous barking are all signs that your child should stay away. Point these out to your youngster.

On the other hand, a dog on a leash with its master may be a safer bet. If the owner has full control and the dog is wagging her tail, your child may approach slowly with an outstretched arm so the animal can sniff his hand. Be sure that the palm is facing down: Dogs that have been disciplined with an open hand may cringe or respond threateningly to the sight of an open hand, even though your youngster has no intention of slapping. Your child should stand still while the animal gets to know his scent. Eventually, she will allow him to pet her.

Because animal bites are relatively common, you need to know how to respond. If your child has been nipped, remain calm. Wash the bite with soap and water and flush it by running cool water over it for two minutes. Unless it was your own dog that did the biting, don't try to catch the animal; you may be unable to handle it yourself. Instead, call for help, and contact your physician if you have any reason to suspect the animal was rabid.

Dogs and Bikes

Although dogs chasing a bike or blocking a cyclist's path can cause spills, kicking an animal away while on the vehicle can cause your child to lose his balance and fall. It's best for him to shout, "Go home!" and hope that the animal retreats.

If the dog appears vicious or is attacking, the National Safety Council suggests that the rider dismount and use the bicycle as a shield. He should also yell for help or yell or whistle to gain the owner's attention. It's smart to avoid riding in areas known for their canine nuisances.

Be Prepared for Earthquakes and Other Natural Disasters

L iving in California, I have become used to earthquakes and the extraordinary havoc they can wreak. Yet earthquakes are but one form of natural disaster. Communities in other states suffer floods, hurricanes, blizzards, and tornadoes. The most frightening aspect of these "acts of God" is our lack of ability to predict or control them. But we can be prepared.

Emergency Supplies You Should Keep on Hand

After every temblor, merchants around California re-stock their shelves with earthquake preparedness kits. Handy as they are, you can easily assemble your own disaster kit at lower cost. The provisions in your kit will serve you well, no matter what surprises Mother Nature cooks up. Keep them in a sturdy, plastic trash can in a cool, dry, and dark place in your garage. Your disaster kit should contain:

- A battery-operated radio and extra batteries. Power and phone lines may be down following a disaster. The radio will instruct you on emergency procedures, evacuation routes, and such. Be sure to rotate batteries periodically and replace them before their expiration date.
- A powerful flashlight or battery-operated lantern and extra batteries. Flashlights that require nine-volt batteries will last many hours.
- A few days' worth of emergency water supplies—at least two quarts of drinking water per person per day. We keep about 10 gallons of bottled water in our garage. Be sure to rotate supplies through your kitchen to keep them fresh.

- You'll need to boil any dubious water for five minutes to purify it. In case you can't do this, have ready a water-purifying kit or chlorine bleach and an eyedropper. Strain polluted water through several layers of paper towel, coffee filters, or clean cloth. Carefully follow directions on the kit or use 16 drops of bleach (a quarter of a teaspoon) per gallon of water. Mix vigorously and allow it to stand for 30 minutes. (Keep in mind that you can drink the water in your hot water heater, your ice maker, and the tank—but *not* the bowl—of your toilet if you haven't put disinfectant into it.

- A wrench to shut off natural gas supply to avoid gas explosions. You can store it by the gas meter.

- A wrench to shut off the water main in case pipes burst.

- Emergency food supplies to last a week. Keep canned foods such as tuna, beans, vegetables, juices, pudding, peanut butter, soups, and dried packaged foods like raisins, crackers, cereal, powdered milk, and granola bars. These should be rotated into your household pantry to keep them fresh. The shelf-life of canned goods is a year.

- A nonelectric can opener.

- A butane camp stove, charcoal barbecue, or Sterno stove for heating foods and boiling water. Do not use these stoves until you've determined there are no gas leaks inside or outside your home. Use the charcoal stove outside only: Burning charcoal gives off carbon monoxide fumes that can be deadly.

- Waterproof matches.

- Blankets, sleeping bags, or aluminum-foil camping blankets.

- A first-aid kit that includes: a first-aid book, antiseptic, bandages, emergency ("quick") ice, and any medications that family members must take. Periodically check to make sure the medications haven't exceeded their expiration date.

- Disposable eating utensils, if you wish, and packaged towelettes for cleanup.

- A working fire extinguisher.

Other Home Preparation

When gas pipelines are broken, one always runs the risk of explosion or fire. Learn in advance how to shut off the gas lines and

electricity to your home. You'll also need properly placed and operating smoke alarms, and, if you live in a multistory dwelling, a
portable fire escape ladder. (See 47, Equip Your Home with Smoke
Detectors and Fire Extinguishers.)

Things to Keep in Your Car

In case disaster strikes when you're away from your home, stow
some supplies in your car trunk. A full disaster preparedness kit may
be impractical, but you should at the very least pack a gallon of
drinking water (rotate for freshness), some flat shoes (in case you're at
work in high heels), and an old coat and blanket, or warm sweaters,
should you and your family have to spend the night out of doors.

Have a Family Plan

For everyone's peace of mind and safety, devise a plan of action
now before the next natural disaster occurs. Here's what you can do:

♦ Teach your children the safe spots in each room of your
  house. If you live in tornado or hurricane country, you
  may have a storm cellar. Children who grow up in
  earthquake-prone states should be taught either to
  crouch under a table or desk or to stand in a doorway or
  hallway, away from glass and windows.

♦ Determine the more dangerous areas in the house and
  take precautions. You might want to bolt your water
  heater to the wall or cover large picture windows with
  sheets of plywood if you've been notified that a twister
  or hurricane is on the way, for instance.

♦ Go over what each family member should do in case of
  emergency.

♦ Have disaster drills to practice the plan. Refine it, if
  need be.

♦ Designate a spot where you should all meet after the
  event, in case you become separated.

♦ Research the emergency situation policy of your child's
  school. To whom and under what circumstances are
  children released? How long will school personnel keep

youngsters at school if parents can't be reached or can't pick them up? Consider establishing an evening program (perhaps through the PTA) to discuss the school's disaster policy.

Phone Tips

Because the telephone could save lives in the moments following a disaster, you should bear these points in mind:

◆ Long-distance lines may be repaired before local lines, so designate an out-of-state friend or relative to act as a clearinghouse for emergency phone calls. Family members should contact that person to report their location and condition. He or she can then relay your messages to other friends or family outside the disaster area. Teach this number to your school-age child.

◆ Don't use phone lines immediately after a disaster. Limit your calls to emergencies only and don't call 9-1-1 or the police for disaster information. Rely on your portable, battery-operated radio.

◆ If you must make an emergency call, it may take several minutes to get a dial tone. Don't click the receiver, since that will only delay your call.

◆ If you get a "fast busy" or a recording that says all circuits are busy, hang up and try again. When phone volume is especially heavy, the phone company may block or divert calls to make sure that emergency personnel can use the lines.

◆ If phone lines are down, it may take hours or even days before calls can be placed.

Helping Your Child Adjust

Although our first concern after a natural disaster is physical safety, we should also take into account our child's emotional well-being. No matter what the disaster, it's likely that your youngster will have a strong emotional reaction to it. Some children regress. Others have difficulty falling asleep or sleeping by themselves. They may suffer nightmares.

If you must leave your home and familiar surroundings for safer ground or more stable housing, your child may feel dislocated, frightened, and confused. It's inevitable that routines will be disrupted. And if you're anxious or upset, he will read your emotions and feel doubly insecure.

Anxiety is a natural reaction to a natural disaster. Just like adults, kids fear that catastrophe will recur and that they will become injured or die. (And in the case of earthquakes, strong aftershocks make this a viable possibility.) In addition, children are terrified of becoming separated from or losing their parents, upon whom they so depend.

To help your child deal with his powerful emotions:

◆ Be reassuring. Show him that the family is safe and together, despite the disaster.

◆ Share your own feelings, encouraging your child to talk about his as much as he needs to. Let him know that doing so will help him feel better. Listen carefully to his fears.

◆ Validate his feelings. You can say, "I see how scared you must be." If you belittle or deny your youngster's emotions, saying, for instance, "There's nothing to be afraid of anymore," he may feel unsupported and even more fearful.

◆ Allow him to draw, paint, or play-act the event.

◆ If your child has a hard time sleeping, you may need to be flexible about bedtime rituals, but return to your normal routine as soon as possible.

◆ Don't criticize or belittle the child who has regressed. Bed-wetting and thumb-sucking are signs of your youngster's anxiety. Be reassuring and ignore these minor setbacks; by drawing negative attention to them, you may prolong them.

◆ If your youngster's fears persist or worsen over time, it's wise to seek psychological help. Your family doctor or pediatrician can guide you to a qualified child counselor. The sooner you treat the problem, the sooner your child will return to normal.

Choose a Day-Care Facility Wisely

When making child-care arrangements for your youngster, you may find it convenient to hire a babysitter (see 5, Find the Best Babysitter and Nanny). However, as your child grows and matures, she may have more fun in an afterschool day-care program. Preschool and school-age youngsters need to interact with peers as they develop their gross and fine motor skills, and interaction in a supervised environment is best.

Before selecting a facility, it's imperative that you visit day-care settings to observe how the children spend their time, whether they seem happy and healthy, and how the staff interacts with them. What follows are specifics you should find in a program that will support your child's physical and emotional well-being.

Health Concerns

The safety measures you take at home should likewise be observed at the day-care facility.

- Make sure there's a clean water supply and working toilets. Is the place clean?
- Does the center serve nutritious snacks?
- Has the caregiver been trained in rescue breathing, CPR, and first aid?
- Are emergency numbers posted by the phone?
- Have medicines, toxic substances, and sharp or dangerous objects been stored out of reach?
- Does the center keep parents' phone numbers on file in case of an emergency?

◆ Do toilet-trained children wash their hands after toileting?
◆ Do staff members wash their hands after taking children to the bathroom?
◆ Do children and staff wash their hands before snacks or meals?
◆ Are tissues available for kids with runny noses? These should be disposed of immediately after use, at which time kids should be trained to wash their hands. (Bear in mind, however, that kids are contagious three to five days before actually becoming ill. Your child may be exposed to illnesses even if the day-care facility requires sick children to stay home.)
◆ What is the center's policy if a child becomes ill during the day? Are sick children isolated?
◆ Do youngsters have their own linens for nap time? These should be laundered regularly.
◆ Does the staff discourage the sharing of snacks and drinks? (It's
 ٠ inadvisable to share because illnesses can be spread in that way.)

Sexual Abuse and Exploitation

According to the National Center for Missing and Exploited Children, the vast majority of day-care centers are safe, loving places. Nevertheless, a child does run the risk of encountering sexual abuse in such settings. To help you ascertain the safety of the facility you are considering, here are some guidelines:
◆ Meet with the staff of the center. Observe how they relate to their charges. Are they respectful of the youngsters' emotions? You might want to meet other adults who will have contact with your child, such as the bus driver or custodian.
◆ Check with the police department and the social services department to see if any complaints have been filed against employees there.
◆ Large centers should be licensed. They should also make criminal-history background checks on their employees. Have they been screened for drug abuse, emotional instability, and child sexual assault? Ask the director about these reports.
◆ *There should be no restrictions on parents coming to the center at any time.* Be suspicious if you must either make an appointment or

call ahead to drop in. Moreover, parents should have access to all areas of the center.

◆ According to the National Center for Missing and Exploited Children, two-thirds of all day-care sexual abuse occurs during toileting. Bathrooms should have no areas in which children could be isolated. Ask who supervises excursions to the toilet.

◆ Children could be vulnerable to abuse during nap time because the majority of classmates will likely be sleeping and the rest of the staff may be out of the room. Ask who supervises naps.

◆ Find out who else will be interacting with your child. According to the National Center for Missing and Exploited Children, in 36 percent of day-care sex-abuse cases, the child was molested by a relative of the care provider.

◆ Be sure to teach your youngster how to handle inappropriate advances made by adults. (See 28, Prevent Sexual Abuse, for more insights.) If you suspect that your child has suffered abuse, follow the guidelines in 29, Know How to Recognize and Respond to the Signs of Sexual Abuse.

Safety of the Day-Care Facility

Along with checking out the staff of a prospective day-care center for your child, you'll want to investigate the surroundings:

◆ Make sure there are no obvious safety hazards, like frayed electrical cords or unprotected hot water pipes.

◆ If the day-care center is home-based, has the swimming pool been properly fenced off? Do child safety latches prevent youngsters from getting to dangerous substances and equipment?

◆ Are there adequate smoke alarms and fire extinguishers with easy access?

◆ Is the playground equipment anchored properly, set either in a bed of wood chips or fine sand? (See 8, Keep Play Equipment Safe.)

◆ Are toys properly maintained?

◆ Do windows have protective guards to prevent falls?

◆ Is the facility well maintained? (Are broken steps repaired, pipes fixed, floors washed, and so forth?)

◆ Ask if the home has been tested for radon, lead paint, asbestos, and impure water. (You can insist on such testing; if environmental pollution is detected, you can ask that they take corrective measures.)

Your Child's Emotional Safety

The safety of your child's surroundings is a central consideration, but the day-care center must also meet your youngster's emotional needs. Look for the following:

◆ Determine the child-to-adult ratio. For young children, 10 to 1 is acceptable. The more workers available, the more attention your youngster will receive.

◆ What is the staff turnover rate? Adults bond to children after working with them for a time. If a facility has a high turnover rate, caregivers don't become so attached to the children. Kids, in turn, become withdrawn. Consistency is key.

◆ Observe how those in charge deal with conflicts among children. They should help children to settle their differences. Do they set limits on behavior and give children "time outs" if they overstep the limits?

◆ Do caregivers discipline the youngsters calmly, or is there a lot of yelling? (If there is, I'd run the other way! Physical punishment is absolutely out of bounds.)

◆ Do the caregivers get down to the child's level to talk to her? Does she or he make eye contact?

◆ How do the caregivers respond to a cranky, whiny child? Do you detect irritation or compassion and patience?

◆ Observe the caregivers' language. Is profanity in evidence? Do they praise children for their efforts? If you hear a lot of criticism, you can be sure a child's self-esteem will be in jeopardy.

◆ Do the caregivers seem happy around children? Do they express love for them?

◆ Do they provide structured activities? Bored children become disruptive and angry. The activities should be complex enough for your child's level of maturity and ability but not so complex that they engender frustration.

◆ Is there a spot to simply flop down and relax? Kids need unstruc-

tured time to rest and to think independently.
- Are there age-appropriate books and toys? Television should not be used as a babysitter.
- Does each child have a cubby to store books, toys, or transitional objects (such as a blankie or Teddy) from home?
- How do caregivers communicate with parents? Can you see them daily and ask about your child's day?
- Are the children happy? You can sense when there's tension among youngsters. If the mood seems chaotic, angry, or bored, I would seek elsewhere.

Watch for Playground Safety

Each year, 150,000 children require emergency medical treatment for playground injuries, according to the federal Consumer Product Safety Commission. Many accidents result from misusing equipment: Walking too close to, standing on, or jumping from swings; balancing in the middle of the seesaw; climbing up the slide rather than the ladder—these can all cause avoidable injuries. It's also of note that some 75 percent of all serious playground injuries result from falls, an estimate provided by the Consumer Federation of America, a nonprofit group.

Clearly, the first step toward playground safety is to teach your youngster how to safely use the equipment.

Swings.

1. Make sure your youngster stays well out of the way of children swinging.

2. While she's on the swing, she should stay seated at all times and hold on with both hands; she should never try to jump from a moving swing.

3. Only one child at a time should ride.

Seesaw.

1. Your child should not try to walk the seesaw plank.

2. She should warn her partner when she's ready to get off so that child can do the same.

3. Both riders must position the board so that it's parallel to the ground before they dismount.

Slides.

1. Slides should be ascended from the ladder side only.

2. Your child should sit on the slide with her arms in her lap as she goes down.

Height and Size Requirements

Research has shown that children are more likely to fall from equipment that is too big for them. The Consumer Federation of America recommends that preschoolers' equipment not exceed six feet in height. School-age children can play on platforms and slides that are seven feet from the ground. Direct your youngster to appropriate playground equipment when you're at the park together.

Check Out the Safety of the Equipment

Because your older school-age child may go to the playground on her own, you can't always supervise her activities. If you can't be absolutely sure she's using the equipment properly, it's wise to make sure that the equipment itself is as safe as it can possibly be.

Playground equipment should be situated on a bed of wood chips or soft sand to break falls. (Refer to 8, Keep Play Equipment Safe, for more details on home playground equipment.) Tests by the Consumer Product Safety Commission show that:

♦ A nine-inch layer of uncompressed wood chips cushions a fall from a seven-foot-high platform.

♦ A six-inch layer of dry uncompressed fine sand (or a nine-inch layer of wet compressed sand) cushions a fall from a five-foot-high platform.

Wet sand can become compacted and hard, as would heavily trafficked lawn and dirt. The deeper the layer of cushioning material, the higher the equipment can be—although injury can occur even in the most protective environment. You should not permit your youngster to use playground equipment set on asphalt or concrete. In fact, if that's all that's available in your community, you would be well advised to complain to city Parks and Recreation authorities.

In addition, check to see that equipment is spaced adequately. If the swings, for example, are too close to a wall, it would force passers-by to come near the swings, and your passing youngster may have to come too close to a swinging child. Also, be sure that ramps and platforms have railings or other such barriers to prevent falls.

Public Bodies of Water

Children should not swim in lakes or ponds, public pools, or the ocean without a lifeguard on duty or, at the very least, a parent in attendance. Your youngster needs to know that she should ask your permission to swim in a public facility and that she should obey all of the lifeguard's directives, including an order to clear the pool or water. For everyone's safety, diving should occur only in designated areas, such as the deep end of the pool or a cordoned-off section. Before diving, your child should jump in feet-first to test the depth of the water.

If your youngster is a weak swimmer, equip him with a certified life vest. Inflatable tubes and rafts are merely toys and cannot be relied upon. Among other things, they puncture easily and therefore are unsafe, especially in ocean waters.

Give your youngster swimming lessons. Three-year-olds are not too young to learn. If your 11- or 12-year-old wants to swim without you, make sure a lifeguard is available and that your child is accompanied by a buddy who also knows how to swim. The buddy can call for help should the need arise. Two quick but critical details: Be sure your child knows to get out of the water if an electrical storm is approaching. The age-old advice not to go into the water 30 minutes after having eaten still applies. Cramps can disable even the strongest swimmer.

PART
IV

Health

Watch

Teach Your Child About Sexuality and Sexually Transmitted Diseases

Did you know that every 13 seconds, a teen in the U.S. gets a sexually transmitted disease and that every 30 seconds a teen becomes pregnant? These problems can easily be avoided by teaching children early on to take the proper precautions.

Although you may consider it premature to discuss the birds and the bees with your preschooler, rest assured that young children do have sexual curiosity. Why else would we find them playing "doctor" with their playmates?

Children learn about sexuality almost from the moment of birth. They pick up cues from how you hold and stroke them, the loving tone of your voice, the feeling of warmth and intimacy when they're in your arms. They observe interactions between you and your spouse and learn about relationships from how you treat each other. Often, this modeling serves as a more forceful teacher than your words.

Let your child take the lead in discussions of sexuality. Welcome "Where did I come from?" questions and answer them straightforwardly. A preschooler is capable of understanding the mechanics of reproduction within the context of a loving relationship. Reading and discussing books about the conception and birth of baby animals and humans can be useful, especially if your family is expecting a new child. *Where Did I Come From?* (Lyle Stuart, 1977), the picture book by Peter Mayle and Arthur Robins, is entertaining and informative and may prove helpful in talking about these topics.

Begin your discussions of sexuality and reproduction early because as children grow they become more curious about these issues and absorb messages from our culture. Although teenagers, on average, begin engaging in sexual intercourse between ages 15½ and 16, children often begin experimenting with sex as early as 12 or 13. A 10-year-old may have been exposed to hours of relatively sexually explicit material on television, gleaning lessons about submissiveness or sexual manipulation you would rather he or she not learn. It's important to watch TV with your kids and comment upon the images they see, especially during music videos.

Besides, depending on their maturation, some fifth- and sixth-graders are impatient to begin "going steady," using makeup, and otherwise acting like little adults. They may experiment with grown-up relationships if their peers are involved in such activities. If at all possible, discourage or at least don't encourage this behavior. There's no need to rush. Your youngster will be an adult for a very long time!

Moreover, some girls begin menstruation as early as age 10. It's important for them to know that they have the potential to become pregnant and for you to hold frank discussions about how to handle boys' advances. Similarly, some boys reach puberty early, too. If yours has, he should be taught to respect females, to act responsibly toward them, and to understand that some girls his age can become pregnant if they're not careful. Teach your daughter not to give mixed messages and your son to appreciate that when a female says no, she means no. These strategies may help prevent future date rapes. *What's Happening to Me?* (Lyle Stuart, 1975), also by Peter Mayle and Arthur Robins, is a humorous and informative guide to puberty and can lend parents and children alike insights into this period of transition.

Depending on your religious or moral beliefs, you may also wish to discuss contraception. Although abstinence is preferable, it is, needless to say, difficult to enforce. Teach your youngster that it's okay to say no and to wait for a long-term, committed relationship before "fooling around." In the event that your child becomes sexually active, however, I believe it preferable and realistic to encourage him or her to use some method of birth control. Unwanted teenage pregnancies cause untold miseries.

It is wise to remind preteens that although birth control pills may block pregnancy, they do nothing to prevent such sexually transmitted diseases (STDs) as AIDS (see 35, Teach Your Child About AIDS), syphilis, gonorrhea, herpes, chlamydia, and venereal warts. The Department of Health and Human Services estimates that 2.5 million teens are infected with STDs. Of course, AIDS is fatal, and syphilis and gonorrhea are life threatening if untreated, but the other diseases can be heartbreaking as well: Chlamydia can cause sterility, herpes can lead to social isolation and threaten the health of newborns, and genital warts can give rise to cervical cancer.

It's better to be safe than sorry: When abstinence is no longer a viable alternative, condoms should always be used—even if a girl is on "the pill." Indeed, certain antibiotics render the birth control pill ineffective (which is why doctors should be informed that a girl takes "the pill"). To paraphrase the 16-year-old son in the newspaper comic strip *For Better or For Worse,* "My driver's license is the second most important thing in my wallet." The most important thing is a condom. It's worth noting that while lots of adolescent males do store condoms in their wallets, condoms can suffer critical damage there. They are safer when stored in a cooler, less jostled place.

Teach Your Child About AIDS

The world certainly has changed. While most of our parents were spared the need of explaining the whys and wherefores of AIDS to us, we have no such luxury when it comes to informing our children. Educating our children about AIDS may be one of the most important things we can do to keep them safe.

AIDS is a growing problem among children. A 1992 report by the Select Committee on Children, Youth and Families disclosed that AIDS cases in the 13-to-24 age range grew 62 percent from 1989 to 1991. Heterosexual contact is the largest source of AIDS among teenage girls. Girls bear a greater risk of contracting AIDS from heterosexual sex than boys because vaginal tissue is more susceptible than the penis to tiny cuts and abrasions from intercourse. If a girl's partner is infected, the virus, carried in his blood and semen, can enter her bloodstream through these cuts. Adolescent boys are more likely to get AIDS from blood transfusions (if they are hemophiliac, for example) and homosexual activity and perhaps from intravenous drug use.

Unfortunately, we cannot depend solely on the government or the schools to do an effective job of teaching children about this terrible disease. According to the Select Committee's report, the federal government's efforts to fight AIDS among our youth is "underfunded, uncoordinated and largely unsuccessful." Only 5 percent of the AIDS-fighting budget is directed toward adolescents, and only 300 schools in the U.S. have health-education programs that run from kindergarten through twelfth grade. Yet, these long-term programs are believed to be the "most promising strategy to reduce risky behavior and promote healthy decisions" among teenagers.

Clearly, you must pick up the ball here, no matter how difficult the subject matter may be. What you say and how you say it will, of course, depend on your child's age and maturation. You don't have to spill all the beans at once. For example, if your elementary-school–age child is not even remotely sexually active and comes in no contact with intravenous (IV) drug users—a group at high risk of contracting AIDS through the dirty needles they share—you can postpone the discussion of sexual transmission or shared syringes until he is older. In fact, a series of discussions over time may be more effective. As your child matures and can handle more information, return to the subject to fill in the details.

The Centers for Disease Control offers the following guidelines about how to approach and what to tell your kids.

How to Start the Conversation

If you feel embarrassed or awkward about bringing up the subject, use the media to help you. Basketball star Earvin "Magic" Johnson's and tennis great Arthur Ashe's recent disclosures that they are HIV positive may be useful to open the door to dialogue. The death of celebrities, such as Freddie Mercury of Queen, or Madonna's appearances for the American Foundation for AIDS Research can also trigger discussion. So might TV programming, ads, or newspaper articles. Your youngster might bring home information from school (you can ask if he has been learning about AIDS) or from the community at large. Your child may simply ask what the fuss is all about. Capitalize on such moments.

Understand Your Role

The Centers for Disease Control suggests that you think of yourself as a counselor, coach, advisor, friend, or guide. Your role is to help your youngster make healthy decisions. If you feel nervous or embarrassed about broaching the subject of AIDS, let your child know. That will ease the tension you both may be feeling. And be sure to have a *dialogue*. If you lecture, your youngster may simply tune you out. Inquire about what he knows concerning AIDS.

Exchange ideas and correct misconceptions, but don't be critical. Do listen to your youngster's fears and concerns.

Know the Facts
You don't have to be an expert to talk to your youngster about AIDS, but you should know the facts. The following should help you in your discussion:

What is AIDS?
AIDS stands for *Acquired Immune Deficiency Syndrome*. It's a disease that breaks down the immune system, inhibiting the body's ability to protect itself from infections and diseases. Actually, people don't die of *AIDS*, per se; they die of the diseases their bodies can't fight off when they get AIDS.

What causes AIDS?
AIDS is caused by the human immunodeficiency virus, also called HIV. A person may have HIV for many years before any symptoms become apparent. You can't tell who is HIV positive just from looking at him or her. What's more, the infected person can pass the virus along to someone else even if he or she doesn't feel or look sick. Nevertheless, an HIV-positive person will eventually develop a full-blown case of AIDS.

How can you tell if you have HIV?
Doctors can detect HIV by taking a blood sample and testing it. An HIV-positive person should be under a doctor's care, even if he doesn't look or feel sick.

Is there a cure for HIV or AIDS?
There are some experimental drugs that may help improve or extend the life of an AIDS patient, but there are no known cures as of yet. The best way to avoid getting sick is to be careful.

How do people get AIDS?
There are several ways to get AIDS:

1. *Sexual intercourse.* HIV can be transmitted during sexual intercourse from male to female, female to male (less common), or male to male. The virus may be in the infected person's blood, semen, or vaginal secretions. It may enter the bloodstream through

tiny cuts and abrasions and can be passed along quickly during sexual intercourse if no precautions have been taken.

2. *Intravenous drug use.* Blood from an infected person can remain on a needle. An uninfected person using the same needle can introduce HIV into his own bloodstream.

3. *Blood transfusions.* In the past, numerous people became infected with HIV from receiving infected blood. Today that's very rare because blood is tested more carefully.

4. *From pregnant mothers.* Women with HIV can give birth to infected babies.

Is it easy to get AIDS?

No. You *cannot* get AIDS from:

◆ Shaking hands, touching, hugging, or kissing an infected person. (Family members who take care of AIDS patients don't get sick.)

◆ Cups, plates, spoons, or other such objects used by AIDS patients.

◆ Toilet seats, door knobs, phones, water fountains, clothes, or mosquito bites.

◆ Sweat, tears, sneezes of an infected person.

◆ Sitting next to or playing with someone who has AIDS.

◆ Donating blood.

How can I protect my child from getting AIDS?

Once your child reaches puberty, you may want to discuss sexual transmission of AIDS, if you haven't already. *Abstinence is the only sure protection.* You might encourage your youngster to say no to sex. Admittedly, enforcing this can be difficult, given our cultural expectations and the nature of peer pressure. To help your child maintain resolve, the Centers for Disease Control suggests that he practice statements such as, "I am just not ready for it yet," or, "I care about you, but I don't want the responsibility that comes with sex."

You should be aware that the use of drugs or alcohol can lower inhibitions and impair a youngster's ability to make healthy choices. Stress to your child that he should never make decisions about sexual relations while under the influence of these substances.

The second-best way for your youngster to protect himself from the sexual transmission of HIV is to create a long-term relationship with one faithful, uninfected partner. The greater the number of sexual partners, the greater the risk of infection. But, even in these circumstances, your child should take precautions.

One primary precaution is using a condom, although some people's religious beliefs may prevent them from doing so. Condoms create a barrier between semen and tissue susceptible to invasion by HIV. If your child decides to use condoms, be sure to explain their proper use. *Make it clear that condoms are not fail-safe. They can break or slide off during intercourse.* The following precautions should be observed:

- Use condoms during every sexual encounter—vaginal, oral, or anal.
- Be sure the condom is made of *latex* rubber. It should say so on the package. Studies suggest that lambskin, or "natural membrane," is too porous.
- Put the condom on as soon as the penis becomes erect.
- Use a spermicide in the tip and all around the condom. The female partner should also apply spermicidal foam or jelly.
- Lubricants should not be petroleum-based because they can cause the condom to break. These include Vaseline, baby oil, cold cream, or cooking shortening.
- Never use a condom more than once.
- Don't use old or brittle condoms or ones that have been exposed to excessive heat.

Finally, your child can help avoid AIDS by refraining from using drugs of any kind, but especially drugs that must be injected. Tell your younger child never to pick up any syringe he may find on the ground. These are to be treated like poison because they can be just as deadly. For organizations that can provide further information on AIDS, see the Resource Guide.

Learn First Aid

The American Red Cross offers myriad classes, brochures, and books that teach the basics of first aid. While we have already covered some first-aid topics, such as what to do in case of poisoning, there are many other issues to be aware of. Let's look at some of them:

◆ **Abrasions and scrapes.** Wash the area thoroughly with soap and warm water. Remove any foreign objects that might have become imbedded in the wound and apply an antiseptic. Cover with sterile nonadhesive gauze, using medical tape (sparingly) to keep the gauze in place. Leave the wound open at night, if possible. Call a doctor if your child may need a tetanus shot (a consideration if he was cut by a rusty object) or if signs of infection, such as swelling, reddening, pain, or oozing pus appear.

◆ **Back or neck injuries.** If your child has sustained a back or neck injury, do not attempt to move her. Dial 9-1-1 or another community emergency service. Moving the victim incorrectly can cause permanent damage and even death.

◆ **Bumps and Bruises.** The American Red Cross recommends that you not use aspirin for pain relief—it can increase internal bleeding. Rather, use acetaminophen (such as Tylenol). In addition, use ICE:

  ◆ Ice, 20 minutes on, 20 minutes off
  ◆ Compression, with an Ace bandage
  ◆ Elevation, above the heart, if possible

◆ **Burns.** You can probably treat first-degree burns (characterized by redness, mild swelling, moderate pain) yourself. Second- and third-degree burns (blisters, wetness, deep tissue destruction, whiteness, or charring) require immediate medical treatment. Flush minor burns with warm running water. Keep the area dry and clean, and cover the injury with sterile nonadhesive gauze. Change the gauze if it becomes wet or dirty. Be alert for signs of infection.

◆ **Cuts.** Control bleeding by putting direct pressure on the area or on the artery between the injury and the heart. Elevate the area above the heart, and use ice to constrict the blood flow. Wash the area with soap and water and apply an antiseptic. Cover the injury with nonadhesive sterile gauze. Keep the area clean and dry, and watch for signs of infection. *If you cannot control the bleeding, if the wound is deep, long, or caused by a dirty object, or if the injury is to the eye area, seek immediate medical attention.*

◆ **Eye injuries.** Don't allow your child to rub his eyes. To remove a foreign object, lift the upper eyelid over the lower one. Allow tears to wash the eye clean. If there is no relief, seek medical attention. If your child has been hit in the eye, apply cold compresses for 20 minutes. Bleeding, discoloration, or continued pain require further medical treatment. If an object has stuck in your child's eye, bandage the eye lightly without undue pressure and seek medical attention immediately.

◆ **Fractures.** Move your child as little as possible. Apply ice and elevate the area. Seek medical attention right away. If you must travel a distance, immobilize the area by splinting it: Put padding on the limb, sandwich the limb between two rigid boards, tying them with strips of fabric.

◆ **Insect bites and stings.** Scrape the stinger out (tweezers may cause more venom to enter the body). Apply ice and compress the area. Clean with soap and water, then use an antiseptic. If your child is having an allergic reaction (hives, itching skin elsewhere, dizziness, difficulty breathing, nausea, vomiting, abdominal pain, swelling of face or tongue, shock, or headache), contact your doctor immediately or call 9-1-1.

◆ **Nosebleeds.** Keep your child calm. Have him sit, leaning forward. Ask him to pinch the tip of his nose, and apply a cold compress. If the bleeding continues, insert a small piece of cotton or gauze into the nostril, leaving some extending from the nose. Resume pinching. Don't let your child blow his nose after the bleeding has stopped. If you can't control the bleeding yourself, seek medical attention. Your physician may cauterize the broken blood vessel.

◆ **Sprains.** Don't allow your child to put any pressure on the sprained area. Avoid aspirin; use acetaminophen (such as Tylenol) instead. Also, use ICE:

   ◆ **Ice,** 20 minutes on, 20 minutes off
   ◆ **Compression,** with an Ace bandage
   ◆ **Elevation,** above the heart, if possible

Seek medical attention if swelling or pain persists, if the area becomes discolored, or if your child heard a snapping or tearing at the time of the accident.

Learn Rescue Breathing, CPR, and the Heimlich Maneuver

Simply reading a book or looking at a diagram about how to administer rescue breathing, CPR, or the Heimlich maneuver is inadequate training. You need hands-on experience for the countless number of situations (near-drownings, choking, allergic reactions) a child can get into. Training will help you feel confident helping your youngster (or any child) in case of an emergency. The American Red Cross offers emergency classes in most communities.

The Red Cross also offers these pointers—what they call "Emergency Action Principles"—on how to deal with emergencies:

1. Survey the scene. Be sure the area is safe; watch for downed electrical lines or other hazards. Try to ascertain what happened and how many people were injured. Look for bystanders who can call 9-1-1 for help.

2. Do a primary survey. The Red Cross calls these the ABCs of emergency care.

A: Airways. If your child is unconscious, check to see if her breathing airway is open. If it's not, tilt the head back.

B: Breathing. Is the victim able to breathe? If not, pinch the youngster's nose and do mouth-to-mouth breathing (for which you should have received training).

C: Circulation. Is the child's heart beating? Is there severe bleeding (blood that spurts with each heartbeat)? If the heart has stopped, administer CPR by compressing and releasing the child's chest rhythmically. Really, you should have CPR training to do this. If the youngster is bleeding severely, apply pressure and elevate the area above the child's heart, if possible.

If a child has problems with her airway, breathing, or circulation, her life is in jeopardy. The brain begins to die after four to six minutes of oxygen deprivation, and the heart will stop if the brain loses function. The purpose of emergency breathing and CPR is to get the blood oxygenated and flowing mechanically until help arrives. CPR does not restart a heart that has stopped beating.

3. Call 9-1-1 or 0 for emergency medical service. If you have been trained in CPR, stay with the child and administer emergency treatment. Have a bystander call for help. He or she should report the location of the accident, the phone number (even of the phone booth from which the call is made), what happened, how many people are injured, whether first aid is being rendered, and the condition of the victim(s). The caller should not hang up until the person at the other end does first.

4. Do a secondary survey. If the child is able to talk, ask what happened. Check breathing, temperature, and pulse and look for other nonlife-threatening injuries. Remain calm and keep the child warm and quiet.

Choking and the Heimlich Maneuver

Children choke due to any number of circumstances. They may inhale a bit of food while giggling, talking, or running; they may swallow small toys, hard candies, or coins that block the air passages; they may try swallowing a piece of food they haven't chewed adequately. A choking child can lose consciousness and die within minutes from lack of oxygen. Signs of choking include:

- Forceful coughing (which signifies a partial blockage).
- Weak coughing or a high-pitched sound coming from the throat (more severe blockage).
- The inability to speak, cough, or breathe (total blockage).
- Grabbing at the throat in panic.
- Unconsciousness.

If your child is coughing forcefully, most likely she will cough up the foreign object. Stay with her and encourage her to continue coughing. If she seems unable to do so, call 9-1-1.

If your child is conscious and experiencing a severe or total blockage, the Red Cross suggests you use the Heimlich maneuver:

◆ Stand or kneel behind your child.
◆ Put your arms around her waist.
◆ Make a fist with your right hand. Put the thumb side against your child's abdomen, in the middle and slightly above the navel but well below the breastbone.
◆ Grab your fist with your left hand and press it into your child's abdomen with quick upward thrusts.
◆ Repeat until your child coughs up the object or goes unconscious. The procedure for an unconscious child is more complex and *requires training*. During a CPR course, you will be taught to roll your youngster on her back, administer abdominal thrusts, check for foreign bodies in the throat with your index and middle fingers, and give slow breaths. If you have not been trained, call 9-1-1 immediately, then do what you can.
◆ Stop thrusting once your child breathes or coughs. Be sure the breathing is not labored. If it is, see your doctor.
◆ The Heimlich maneuver itself can cause other injuries. Call 9-1-1 and have your child taken to the emergency room even after she is breathing once more.

The best defense against choking is eliminating situations in which it can occur:

◆ Cut your youngster's food into bite-size pieces that cannot lodge in her throat.
◆ Keep an eye on your child when she eats. If she becomes too excited or animated, she may eat too quickly and choke on her food.
◆ Don't allow your youngster to run around while eating.
◆ Be sure that no small objects like coins, beads, marbles, or hard candies are within your young child's reach. Be sure to clean under beds and sofa cushions regularly. Get down to floor level and observe if any questionable objects might have inadvertently fallen under furniture. These may be hard for you to get at yet within your

youngster's reach.

◆ Make sure toys are in good working order. Stuffed animals' eyes should be tightly secured. Small, swallowable game pieces can be dangerous.

◆ If you suspect that your preschooler has put something in her mouth, have her spit it out immediately.

Be Realistic About Illnesses

Any time a child enters a new child-care or school environment, he is exposed to a new raft of germs. It's inevitable that kids entering preschool, kindergarten, or even junior high will become ill more frequently until they have built up an immunity to the unfamiliar microbes.

Nevertheless, it's important to bear in mind that children get sick year-round whether or not they're in school. According to the Child Care Action Campaign, a New York-based child-care advocacy group, preschoolers who are cared for at home (and thus exposed to fewer germs) average six to eight upper-respiratory illnesses and one or two gastrointestinal illnesses yearly. Kids who are cared for in a child-care facility have the same number of colds but may have twice as many stomach flus.

In 32, Choose a Day-Care Facility Wisely, I cover ways that a child-care facility can prevent the spread of illness among its young charges. Remember, however, that kids are contagious at least three to five days before they develop symptoms. Merely keeping a sick child home may be akin to closing the barn door after the cows have escaped.

Other than following the guidelines I've suggested, especially those regarding food sharing, hand washing, and tissue disposal, there's not a whole lot you can do. But you should know when it's advisable to keep your youngster home from school. The Child Care Action Campaign suggests that a child be isolated from playmates under the following circumstances:

◆ He has fever. He may complain of the chills or hotness. He may

have a stiff neck or feel lethargic. My kids were in the habit of vomiting whenever their temperature exceeded 100°F. Fun!
- He has diarrhea. Persistent diarrhea (five or more defecations in an eight-hour period) can cause dehydration. Blood or mucus in the stool is also of concern. If a child has been diagnosed with shigella, salmonella, giardiasis, or campylobacter, he should be isolated for 24 hours after the diarrhea stops or 24 hours after treatment, on your doctor's recommendation.
- He vomits or has diarrhea three times or more.
- He is contagious with measles, German measles, mumps, chicken pox, whooping cough, or diphtheria.
- He has a persistent and severe sore throat, a sore throat with swollen glands, or a sore throat accompanied by a red body rash. (These may indicate strep throat.)
- He has head or body lice.
- He has a rash that has not been diagnosed.
- He has persistent or intermittent stomach pains.
- He has difficulty breathing.
- He feels lethargic or cries excessively.
- His temperature is over 102°F an hour after you've given him aspirin or acetaminophen (Tylenol) to reduce his fever.

If it were up to me, I would also contact the doctor or bring the child in for treatment. Kids are bound to get sick—there's no foolproof way to keep them safe from the common cold. But by keeping your child home and seeking prompt medical attention, you'll help to insure that the illness stays mild and that it resolves quickly.

Protect Against Food Poisoning

I t is estimated that as many as 4 million Americans annually suffer from the fever, stomachaches, vomiting, and diarrhea that accompany poisoning caused by salmonella bacteria. In some cases salmonella can be fatal. Botulism, too, can cause gastric distress and in severe cases, death. Children are among the most vulnerable.

There's no point in risking your family's health when food poisoning can be easily avoided. A favorite expression in our kitchen has been, "When in doubt, throw it out." Moldy cheese, fruits, and vegetables; leftovers that smell a bit "off"; cans with bulging lids or weeping seams; salsa that's bubbling like champagne…these all get tossed.

Sometimes, however, the bacteria that cause food poisoning aren't so easily detected with the eye or nose. Poultry and eggs may be infected with salmonella without your knowing it. Fish may be contaminated with high levels of bacteria or pollutants. Food preparations, such as garlic preserved in oil, can provide the necessary setting for the toxin-producing botulism bacteria.

How to Prevent Food Poisoning

What's needed is a bit of care and forethought in the kitchen. You'll find the following tips helpful:

To Prevent Botulism
- Heat food to a temperature of at least 176° F for 10 to 15 minutes. Reheat food that has been allowed to cool after cooking.

♦ Don't give your child tastes of food unless it's thoroughly cooked.

♦ Don't let your child eat leftovers that haven't been refrigerated or reheated properly.

Poultry Precautions

Americans consume approximately 17.5 million pounds of chicken a year. Recently, however, much has been written about contaminated chickens. A *Los Angeles Times* survey, for example, found that up to 80 percent of all chickens approved by the U.S. Department of Agriculture (USDA) were infected with bacteria— including salmonella, camphylobacter jejuni, and listeria monocyogenes—that cause food poisoning. To keep your child safe from dangerous poultry:

♦ Bring the chicken right home from the market. Don't let it sit in a hot car for hours, and cook or refrigerate it immediately.

♦ Eat, freeze, or throw away the bird by the expiration date on the package.

♦ Rinse poultry thoroughly under cool water before cooking.

♦ Cook the bird thoroughly. Juices should be clear.

♦ See to it that juices from raw poultry do not mingle with uncontaminated foods.

  ♦ Wash all utensils, cutting surfaces, and plates with soapy, hot water after they've had contact with raw poultry.

  ♦ Wash your hands thoroughly with soapy, hot water after handling the bird and before touching other foods.

  ♦ Avoid using wooden cutting blocks, which can harbor harmful bacteria from raw poultry. If you do use one, soak it in hot water and bleach to kill any salmonella bacteria.

  ♦ Don't baste a barbecued chicken with the marinade in which it had been soaking prior to cooking. Use fresh sauce.

♦ Defrost chickens and turkeys in the refrigerator.

♦ Refrigerate cooked poultry no more than two hours after preparation.

◆ Turkey stuffing that's allowed to sit in a turkey as it's cooking can harbor bacteria. Bake the stuffing in a separate pan.

Be Eggstra Careful Around Eggs

Just as chicken has come under recent scrutiny, so have eggs. In 1990, there were 2,000 reported cases of salmonella stemming from raw eggs. Take the following precautions to avoid egg-related food poisoning:

◆ Eat well-cooked eggs: hard-boiled or scrambled. Soft-boiled, poached, sunny-side up, and even over-easy eggs can harbor the salmonella bacteria because the yolks haven't been cooked sufficiently to kill the microbe.

◆ Avoid foods containing raw egg yolks, such as Caesar salad (unless you insist it be prepared without the egg), homemade mayonnaise, béarnaise and hollandaise sauces, eggs Benedict, and uncooked custards and mousses that contain raw eggs.

◆ Sandwiches and salads (macaroni, tuna, chicken, turkey) containing mayonnaise should be refrigerated at all times.

◆ Some corporations (Hyatt Hotels, Burger King, and United and American airlines) have turned to pasteurized liquid eggs. The low-cholesterol egg products on the market may make a suitable substitute.

There's Something Fishy Going On Here

A February 1992 report by Consumers Union found that nearly half the fish they tested were "contaminated by bacteria from human or animal feces, most likely the result of poor sanitation practices at one or more points in the fish-handling process." In addition, fish spoils when it's allowed to become too warm. When properly handled and refrigerated, most fish stays fresh from 7 to 12 days after it has been taken from the water. How can you tell if the fish you're serving is fresh? *Consumer Reports* offers the following suggestions:

◆ When buying whole fish, make sure the gills are bright red and moist. Avoid fish with brown, mucousy, or clumped gills.

- Check the eyes. They should be clear, bright, and bulging. Cloudy, sunken, or slimy eyes indicate spoilage.
- Check the skin. It should be covered with a translucent mucus and should be bright. Discolored, torn, or blemished skin and sticky brownish-yellow mucus indicate spoilage.
- Check the flesh of fish steaks and fillets. It should be translucent and moist. If it's dry or pulling apart, it may be too old.
- Check the display. Fish shouldn't be in open displays or piled too high on a bed of ice (only the bottom layer of fish will stay cold). There should be no hot lights shining on them, either.
- Don't buy cooked seafood that's displayed next to raw fish. Bacteria from the uncooked fish can contaminate the other.
- Refrigerate the fish as soon as you bring it home and use it within a day or freeze it.
- As with chicken, wash all surfaces with hot, soapy water after they've come in contact with fish.
- Cook the fish thoroughly. Bacteria and parasites can contaminate raw fish, which is why sushi can be risky.

Develop Healthful Eating Habits

As children, we all learned about the four basic food groups: meat, fruits and vegetables, dairy, and breads. Usually these were arranged in a sort of pie chart. Today, the USDA, in recognition that not all foods in a particular group hold the same health values, has devised a new way to envision healthful eating: the food pyramid.

At the base of the pyramid (the largest category) are complex carbohydrates, such as breads, pasta, cereals, and whole-grains like brown rice, barley, and wheat with bran. The government recommends 6 to 11 servings of these a day. On the next level, we find fruits and vegetables. The recommendation here is three to five servings of vegetables and two to four of fruit. Above that level, you'll find proteins, split into dairy and meat. Ideally, we are to consume two to three servings of milk, cheese, or yogurt and two to three servings of meat, poultry, fish, dried beans, nuts, or eggs daily. At the apex of the pyramid are sugars and fats. These your family should consume sparingly.

Helping Your Child Eat Right

Good eating habits are instilled early. As with other behavior, your child will learn by imitating you. If you want your youngster to develop good eating habits, you may need to examine your own. Do you grab a doughnut and coffee and run for the door in the morning? Do you binge on sweets and ice cream? Do you rely on fast foods and frozen prepared meals at dinnertime? Many of these products are high in sugar, fat, sodium, or all three. Indeed, according to the faculty of the UCLA School of Public Health, the average American eats about one-third of a pound of sugar *daily.* About 70 percent of that sugar lies hidden in processed foods.

The eating habits your child develops at an early age can last a lifetime, affecting his health and longevity. The roots of coronary heart disease, for instance, can be traced to childhood eating patterns. About 5 percent of American children between ages 5 and 18 have dangerously high cholesterol levels (more than 200 to 220 mgs/dl). What can you do to ensure your child eats right? You'll find the following suggestions helpful:

◆ Make sure your child eats three nutritious meals a day. Youngsters need to eat before going to school, or they won't have enough energy for the rigors of education.

◆ Cut down on (or eliminate) fatty and salty foods. The American Heart Association recommends that no more than 30 percent of the day's calories come from fat. Fatty foods such as bacon, chips, and french fries have little nutritive value. Serve these sparingly, if at all. Remember, fat in the diet contributes to heart disease and various cancers, and high salt intake can correlate with high blood pressure.

◆ Keep healthful snacks on hand. My kids used to love eating "ants on a log"—a stalk of celery stuffed with peanut butter and studded with raisins. Keep plenty of both fresh and dried fruit and carrot sticks available for snacking. This is not to say that you should eliminate sweets altogether: Children who feel deprived tend to binge. Moderation is the key.

◆ Avoid soft drinks. Your child will be better off if he doesn't develop a soda habit, especially early on. Pure fruit juices (not "fruit drinks") can be more healthful, but beware: The juice of a fruit, such as an apple, has far fewer nutrients (and fiber) than the fruit itself. Milk provides many more nutrients and without the sugar and caffeine of colas. If you're concerned about your family's fat intake, buy low-fat (1 or 2 percent) milk. This does not apply to babies, who need whole milk for proper growth and development.

◆ Cut down on cheese and fatty red meat. Cheese (other than low-fat cottage cheese and some of the new low-fat cheeses) and fatty red meat are high in cholesterol. Your child can obtain calcium from low- or nonfat milk products, such as yogurt, and protein from other sources, like skinless broiled chicken, lean beef, bean soups, and fish. Water-packed tuna has 85 percent less fat than tuna packed in oil. The American Heart Association recommends that daily cholesterol intake be 100 mg of cholesterol per 1,000 calories (not to exceed 300 mg of cholesterol) daily.

◆ Get your youngster used to whole-grain breads before he has the opportunity to develop a preference for white bread. While white bread may be fortified with vitamins and minerals, it lacks the fiber of whole-grain products. Fiber helps maintain intestinal regularity as well as fight colon cancer and heart disease. (A caveat here: Some high-fiber products, such as bran muffins and granola, may also be high in fat and sugar. It's important to study ingredient labels to determine if the product is healthful.)

◆ Encourage your child to eat vegetables, especially dark green, leafy vegetables like spinach and those in the cruciferous family, such as broccoli, cauliflower, cabbage, and brussels sprouts. Cruciferous vegetables provide essential nutrients and help prevent cancer. My younger daughter has taken a distinct disliking to these vegetables but doesn't mind broccoli in Chinese food. Consequently, we frequently prepare vegetables by stir-frying.

◆ If you must use oils, limit yourself to olive or canola oil for cooking. These do not contribute to cardiovascular disease. Butter is high in cholesterol. Other oils such as safflower, sunflower, and corn oil may negate the positive effects of "good" high-density lipoprotein (HDL) cholesterol. Avoid any product that has hydrogenated oil, since this has saturated fat. You might also try low-fat vegetable cooking sprays or even sautéing in a tablespoon of water.

◆ Read labels at the supermarket to find the nutritional values of the products you're considering. Be aware that listed serving sizes may be smaller than what you would consider a normal portion and that claims like "low-fat" or "lite" can be deceiving.

◆ Pay attention to sodium content listed on the label. Too much sodium in the diet can contribute to high blood pressure. The American Heart Association recommends consuming no more

than 2,400 mg daily. Sodium can hide in processed foods and
condiments.
◆ The government recommends that only 20 to 30 percent of your
   daily calories come from fat. Recently such claims as "light," or
   "lite," and "low-fat" have been emblazoned on product labels.
   While these products may have fewer calories or less fat than their
   predecessors, those claims don't guarantee you're buying a product
   that derives fewer than 30 percent of its calories from fat. The
   UCLA School of Public Health suggests that you bring a calcula-
   tor with you to the market to figure out the calorie-fat ratio in
   each product. Here's what to do:
   ◆ The fat will be listed on the label in grams as "fat per
      serving."
   ◆ Multiply that number by 9 (there are 9 calories per fat
      gram). That total is how many calories come from fat in
      this product.
   ◆ Divide the total by the number of calories per serving as
      listed on the label. That will give you the percent of
      calories that come from fat.
   Once you have determined the percentage of fat in a product,
you can make an informed choice regarding whether you want to
purchase or consume it.

Protect Your Child from the Sun

The depletion of the ozone layer has made it increasingly dangerous for adults and children alike to spend time in the sun. Too much exposure to the sun's ultraviolet (UV) rays causes skin cancer. Sunbathing, which once seemed a simple and innocent pleasure, may now be a thing of the past.

Most children are not sun worshippers, but they do spend lots of time playing outdoors. Even if the sky is overcast, as much as 85 percent of the sun's UV rays can penetrate the clouds. Moreover, sun reflecting on the surface of pool, lake, or ocean water, or even snow, can create a nasty burn. How can you keep your child safe?

Understand the Risk Factors
- Fair-haired, light-skinned, freckled, light-eyed people (often of Celtic heritage) are at greatest risk for skin cancer.
- Children who sunburn easily and have a hard time tanning are at risk.
- Children who have suffered a *severe* sunburn accompanied by considerable blistering are at greater risk for melanoma, the most deadly kind of skin cancer.
- By the time a child reaches age 18, she will have received 50 to 80 percent of the sun she'll receive in her lifetime. As adults, we generally spend less time in the sun.

What You Can Do
While you may remember to apply sunscreen at poolside or on the beach, bear in mind that children are frequently exposed to the

sun's UV rays all day long just playing with their friends.

◆ Make it a habit to apply sunscreen to your child's sensitive skin, even if she's just playing out in the yard.

◆ Apply the lotion 30 to 45 minutes before exposure.

◆ Use a sunscreen with a Sun Protection Factor (SPF) of at least 15. Some children's sunscreens have an SPF of 30 or more. Also, check the label to make sure it protects against UVB and UVA rays.

◆ Apply it liberally and evenly over all exposed skin, including the outer ear.

◆ Reapply lotion after swimming or strenuous activity. Certain brands of lotion, such as Bullfrog and PABA-free DuraScreen, are waterproof and thus may last longer.

◆ If your child's nose has a tendency to burn, cover it with zinc oxide ointment. Recently, manufacturers have come out with brightly colored zinc oxide creams that your child can regard as face paint.

◆ Insist that your youngster wear a hat and protective clothing: a baseball cap with a wide brim can protect the face; for the torso, a light T-shirt over a bathing suit—even if your child is in the pool or ocean—will suffice.

If Your Child Has a Sunburn

Take the following precautions:

◆ Keep her out of the sun.

◆ Run cool water over the sunburned area.

◆ Wash the area carefully if blisters appear.

◆ Antiseptic sprays meant for sunburns may help reduce pain and infection.

◆ Have your child drink plenty of fluids.

◆ Watch for infection (redness, swelling, oozing pus).

◆ Give aspirin to reduce pain and inflammation.

Protect Your Child from Mercury Poisoning

Mercury poisoning can cause tremors, nerve damage, anxiety, and kidney disease. Children exposed as fetuses to even low doses of mercury can suffer from developmental delays in walking and talking as well as severe brain damage.

What makes mercury poisoning difficult to fight is the nature of its sources. Mercury vapors in the air can enter the food chain via acid rain. It can also enter the food chain when fish eat plants or smaller fish that have absorbed mercury in rivers downstream from industrial polluters, such as paper mills or smelters.

While mercury in our air is usually too diluted to pose a problem, mercury in water can combine with other elements to form the organic compound *methylmercury*, which can dissolve in animal fat and enter our bloodstream after we ingest that fat.

Methylmercury is less toxic to fish than to humans. It can accumulate in their flesh without our being aware of it. The longer the exposure, the greater the accumulation, so old, large fish—commonly swordfish, tuna, and shark—tend to have higher mercury levels. Indeed, in a recent Consumers Union survey, 90 percent of their swordfish sample had detectable levels of mercury.

To keep your child safe from mercury poisoning, try to find out where the fish you buy was caught. The following guidelines, recommended in the March 9, 1991, issue of *Science News* may help:

♦ The National Fisheries Contaminant Research Center
in La Crosse, Wisconsin, advises that dangerous
methylmercury levels have been detected in brook and
brown trout, small- and largemouth bass, yellow and

European perch, pumpkinseed sunfish, and walleye and
northern pike.

◆ Twenty-one states issue advisories about which fish
taken from which bodies of water are unsafe to eat. Pay
attention to these advisories.

◆ Smaller, younger fish are safer. Methylmercury accumu-
lates in fish over time, so the less time a fish is in water,
the less mercury.

◆ The larger and deeper the lake, the lower the
methylmercury concentration in its fish.

◆ Bottom-feeding fish, like suckers, are less contaminated
than top-feeding game fish, like largemouth bass.

◆ Fish caught in reservoirs older than 20 to 30 years have
higher concentrations of methylmercury.

◆ If you're pregnant, you might want to stick with saltwa-
ter fish that has been designated safe. Oceanic fish like
tuna and shark can accumulate large concentrations of
methylmercury, but they also contain selenium, which
can counteract methylmercury toxicity.

Mercury in Fillings

At least 100 million Americans have silver amalgam dental fillings. In 1990, a ballyhoo was raised over speculation that the filling
material could cause kidney difficulties and other health problems in
humans, as it does in laboratory animals. Experts have known since
1979 that mercury can leach from fillings, and later research has
established that body tissue can absorb some of the escaped mercury.
Nevertheless, the American Dental Association (ADA) asserts that
such small amounts of this metal as are used in fillings do not create
physiological problems in humans and should not be cause for alarm.

Indeed, according to the ADA's "Principles of Ethics and
Professional Code of Conduct," "the removal of amalgam restora-
tions from the nonallergic patient for the alleged purpose of removing toxic substances from the body, when such treatment is per-
formed solely at the recommendation of the dentist, is improper and
unethical."

The mercury in our fillings is combined with other metals, such as silver, tin, and copper, to create a biologically inactive substance. Although tiny amounts of mercury can be absorbed into the body, to date, there is no scientific evidence that this has a toxic effect. In fact, the ADA asserts that removing old amalgam fillings for the sake of eliminating potential toxicity exposes one to more risk:

◆ A sound tooth can be damaged during the removal of a filling, thus requiring a larger filling.

◆ The tooth's nerve could be damaged, and the tooth might be lost.

◆ Replacements for the traditional amalgam are not as sturdy and may break down sooner, thus necessitating larger fillings in the future.

◆ The high degree of mercury vapor that's released in the removal of an old filling can be more dangerous than leaving the filling in place.

To keep your child safe, it's best to discuss with his dentist the risks of using these amalgam fillings. She should be up to date on current research on the subject. Furthermore, if old fillings need to be drilled out to make way for new ones, your dentist should use a "rubber dam" to prevent your child from swallowing stray bits of amalgam. Even though the mercury is bound up in the alloy, there's every reason to play it safe.

PART
V

Substance

Abuse

Prevention

Stop Smoking and Keep Your Child from Smoking

An automated billboard sponsored by the American Heart Association, the American Cancer Society, and the American Lung Association at an intersection near my home counts the number of smoking-related deaths each year. In the amount of time it takes for a red light to turn green (two minutes?), at least one more victim is added to the morbid tally. The facts about smoking are appalling:

- The number of smokers in the country has not declined, despite people quitting or dying from the habit. Fifty million Americans smoke 1.6 billion cigarettes daily. The tobacco industry needs to convince more than 10,000 children *a day* to begin smoking in order to replace the 390,000 to 435,000 smokers who die annually as a result of their addiction.
- More people die from smoking each year than from AIDS, car accidents, suicides, and homicides combined. Smoking is responsible for one of every six deaths in the U.S. (A recent survey in Oregon showed that smoking was responsible for one in four deaths in that state.)
- Nonsmokers live an average of nine years longer than smokers.
- Cigarette smoking is the number-one cause of cancer death in men and women. (A male smoker over the age of 35 is 22 times more likely to die of lung cancer than a nonsmoker. A female smoker over 35 who takes birth control pills runs many other health risks, including cancer.)
- Nicotine, like heroin and cocaine, is highly addictive.
- Tobacco companies spend $5,000 per minute on advertisements

and promotion. Cigarettes are the most heavily advertised products in the country.
- Smoking-related health care and lost productivity cost this nation
  $65 billion a year. That's $262 per person annually.
- Cigarette smoke is also responsible for emphysema and chronic
  bronchitis deaths as well as strokes, heart disease, and cancers
  other than lung cancer.
- A 1986 survey of high school seniors who smoked shows that one-
  fourth began using cigarettes by *sixth grade.* Other studies show
  that 60 percent of smoking teens begin by the age of 14 and 90
  percent by 19.
- In a 1991 national survey of 49,500 junior high and high school
  students, 44 percent of eighth-graders had tried cigarettes, and two
  thirds of the seniors had experimented with them. Half the
  eighth-graders in this survey believed that smoking one or more
  packs a day posed little health risk.
- Cigarette smoke contains about 4,000 chemicals, including 200
  poisons, such as DDT, arsenic, hydrogen cyanide, formaldehyde,
  and carbon monoxide, and 40 known carcinogens.
- Nicotine is so toxic it has been used as an insecticide.
- Secondhand smoke can be more toxic than firsthand. It has twice
  the tar and nicotine and three times the carbon monoxide of
  smoke inhaled through a filter. According to the American Heart
  Association, secondhand smoke kills 54,000 Americans a year. It is
  the third-largest preventable cause of death in the U.S.
- Babies born of pregnant mothers who smoke are smaller and have
  a greater chance of dying soon after birth. As fetuses, they receive
  less oxygen and fewer nutrients because of their mother's
  addiction.
- Pregnant mothers who smoke have a higher rate of both stillborn
  and premature babies as well as miscarriages than nonsmokers.
- Children of smoking parents have twice the incidence of pneumo-
  nia, acute and chronic bronchitis, and other upper-respiratory ail-
  ments. Their brain cancer rate is higher, too.
- In a study of children between the ages of five and nine, it was found
  that those whose parents smoked had impaired lung function.

- Smoking aggravates children's asthma and can trigger an attack.
- Smoking parents become ill more frequently and cough more as a result of their addiction, thereby infecting their children as well.

Why Do Children Start Smoking?

Despite these terrible facts, droves of youngsters continue to take up smoking. The recent controversy about "Joe Camel," the mascot for Camel cigarettes, helps underscore how pervasive and effective the tobacco industry has been in getting its message across to our youth: Joe Camel is as familiar to young children as Mickey Mouse!

Children begin succumbing to the pressure to smoke as they approach adolescence. For years, they have been bombarded with media campaigns showing young and attractive couples lighting up and enjoying themselves. Preteens are just beginning to become autonomous and to establish their own identities; they may wish to emulate these images.

In addition, boys might view smoking as a sign of maturity, rebellion, and macho risk-taking. Girls may view smoking as a means of weight control or, again, as a sign of maturity. Teenagers can use smoking as a sign of their independence. When confronted, they can become defensive and make statements such as, "It's my body, and I'll do what I want with it."

Adolescents rarely believe in their own mortality. If they are to die from cigarette-related causes they perceive that this will occur many years hence. If you're living for the moment, as many adolescents do, it's hard to visualize coping with cancer at age 50. Health warnings have little effect on teenagers.

Peers exert great influence on preteens. Smoking may be what it takes to be part of the "in" crowd. According to the American Heart Association, children who smoke are likely to have friends and older siblings who are also smokers. Additionally, children of smokers are at much greater risk of becoming smokers themselves than children of nonsmokers. The paraphernalia of smoking—ashtrays, lighters, packs of cigarettes—may be strewn around the house. Kids can incorporate these into their unconscious as a normal part of everyday adult life. Even nonsmoking parents whose friends drop by and smoke can convey the subtle message that this is an acceptable social activity.

Ironically, the antismoking programs established by tobacco companies—far from discouraging cigarette use—often insidiously encourage children to pick up the habit by pointing out that it's an "adult choice." If you tell a youngster he's too young to smoke, that it's an activity reserved only for grown-ups, he'll look upon the habit as something to which he should aspire.

What Can You Do?

There are many ways to keep your child from experiencing the destructive effects of tobacco. The first line of defense is to stop smoking yourself. In truth, once a woman becomes pregnant, she should both quit smoking and keep away from secondhand smoke. That may mean her mate should stop smoking too. Not only will these responsible parents spare their child the damage caused by tobacco, but they'll also make smoking a more foreign experience. It's awfully hard to convince a child to "Do as I say, not as I do," when it comes to smoking. Preteens and teenagers are always on the lookout for hypocrisy, especially in their parents.

There are other precautions you can take, as well:

◆ Do not allow smoking in your home, even if it means offending your friends. (In our home, we ask smokers to take their cigarettes outside on the patio.)

◆ Do not allow your preteen or teenager to smoke in the house. It sets a bad example for your younger children. By sending them out, you're conveying the message that smoking is unacceptable. Besides, why make it easy on them?

◆ Do not allow your child to smoke in your presence, even if you're both out of the home.

◆ See to it that your child's school does not permit smoking on campus. Schools that have "smoking zones" have 25 percent more smokers than those that ban smoking.

◆ Rather than focusing on health hazards, point out to your youngsters that smoking makes them unattractive to members of the opposite sex: It yellows their teeth, gives them bad breath, and causes their clothes and hair to smell.

◆ Emphasize how smoking impairs a young athlete's abilities to compete.

◆ Do what you can to discover if your child's friends are smokers, especially if your child smokes: It's harder to beat the habit if you're constantly among other smokers.

◆ Point out to your youngster how the tobacco companies have been manipulating young minds. Perhaps you'll spark his sense of righteous indignation.

◆ Don't give up after one talk. Kids need to hear about smoking over and over again.

◆ If your child smokes, inform his pediatrician or doctor. You may also wish to let a trusted clergyperson or counselor know. These individuals have experience talking with young people about smoking.

◆ Never involve your youngster in your own smoking habit by sending him to buy cigarettes for you (which is illegal in most states, anyway) or by asking him to retrieve or light your cigarettes.

◆ The American Lung Association suggests the following steps you (or your child) can take to stop smoking. But remember, a person has to *want* to stop for these to be effective.

  ◆ Set a quitting date.
  ◆ Remove all smoking paraphernalia from the home, car, locker.
  ◆ Keep low-calorie snacks handy.
  ◆ Spend more time in no-smoking environments like your home, the movies, the library, or a department store.
  ◆ Tell friends and family you're going to stop smoking.
  ◆ Plan other activities to take the place of smoking.
  ◆ Call a nonsmoker friend for support.
  ◆ Contact your local branch of the American Lung Association for help.

Your family doctor can also recommend smoking cessation programs or may even prescribe nicotine gum or a nicotine patch. Different programs work for different people, and several may be tried before one that works for you is found.

Prevent Alcohol Abuse

A lcohol is the leading cause of death among teenagers—not because of the usual alcohol-related diseases connected to long-term use (these include cirrhosis of the liver, heart disease, high blood pressure, stomach ulcers, brain damage, and mouth, esophagus, or stomach cancer)—but because of alcohol-related traffic accidents. More than one-third of all alcohol-induced crashes involve people between the ages of 16 and 24.

Alcohol depresses the nervous system. It impairs one's judgment, coordination, vision, and speech. It can also cause nausea, vomiting, dizziness, and, when consumed to the extreme, unconsciousness, respiratory failure, and death. Chronic alcoholism can shorten one's life by 10 to 12 years.

Alcohol is addictive. The more one drinks, the greater one's tolerance, and the more difficult it becomes to control one's consumption.

Why Do Children Begin Using Alcohol?

Since adults have the legal right to drink and often do so in the presence of their youngsters, preadolescents may perceive alcohol consumption as a sign of maturity or autonomy. In addition, they may be:

◆ Curious. They want to know what all the fuss is about.
◆ Subject to peer pressure. Above all else, preteens need to feel that they belong. If their friends drink, they may believe they must too in order to be part of the "in" crowd.
◆ Insecure. Drinking might help them gain "respect" from their peers or give them fleeting moments of confidence while under

the influence.

- Bored. Drinking provides a momentary high and is seen as entertaining. Beer ads, for example, depict sexy drinkers having enormous fun.
- In emotional pain. Drinking is a way to temporarily numb oneself from loneliness, rejection, criticism, stress, or failure.
- Defiant. Drinking can be an act of rebellion against parents, teachers, or school administrators.
- Lacking in information or values. Children may be unaware of the harmful effects of liquor, or they may not value their own health and well-being.
- Easily influenced. They may model their behavior after parents, older siblings, family friends, or favorite rock idols and movie stars who drink.

How Can You Tell If Your Child Is Drinking?

Your child will leave subtle clues if he's drinking. Ask yourself the following questions:

- Is he acting drunk—slurring words, walking with wobbly and uneven footsteps, displaying impaired coordination?
- Are his eyes bloodshot? Does he wear sunglasses in the house or during class?
- Is he disheveled and poorly groomed?
- Does he experience periods of depression or moodiness—sudden bursts of rage, for example—that he can't explain?
- Has he withdrawn from the family and his usual friends or from school participation?
- Does he have new friends whom he has refused to introduce to you?
- Has he lost interest in favorite hobbies and sports?
- Have his grades dropped?
- Has he been reprimanded for sleeping in class?
- Does he have difficulty concentrating? Is his short-term memory fuzzy?

◆ Has he developed a behavior problem in school?
◆ Have you noticed that money or the family's liquor supply has been disappearing?
◆ Have you found a stash of liquor in his room or unfamiliar liquor bottles and beer cans in the trash?
◆ Do his friends drink?

How to Prevent Your Child from Abusing Alcohol

The pull of peer pressure becomes increasingly forceful as your child nears adolescence. But you can work with your youngster to help prevent his becoming involved in alcohol abuse. The following are some steps you can take:

1. Educate yourself. Take the time to learn about alcohol and other drugs that kids abuse (see 45, Watch for Use of Marijuana and Other Drugs.) What are the signs and the consequences of use?

2. Open the lines of communication. Talk with your youngster about alcohol and drug abuse. Explain that although drinking seems "cool," it's actually dangerous. Be prepared to answer your child's questions, including those about your own alcohol consumption.

3. Be supportive. Let your child know that you understand the pressure he feels to be part of the drug culture.

4. Be firm. Kids feel safe when parents set reasonable limits. In the case of alcohol, it's reasonable for you to explain to your child that you won't allow him to become involved in such harmful activities, but that you'll help him find ways to avoid drinking.

5. Assess your own behavior. As in so many other instances, children model their behavior after their parents'. Parents who abuse liquor set an example for their child. Ask yourself what kind of a model you'd like to be and stick to your commitment—for your child's sake.

6. Help your child develop high self-esteem. Kids who feel good about themselves are less apt to succumb to peer pressure. Pay attention to how you speak to your child—with praise or criticism? Give positive reinforcement for a job well done. Give your youngster responsibilities. For instance, allow him to manage his own allowance. Express an interest and become involved in his activities.

Have reasonable expectations that will help your youngster feel successful. Make yourself available to talk over his problems with him. Express your love and affection.

7. Educate your child. Teach him about the consequences of alcohol abuse. Be sure, even if he's below driving age, that he understands the dangers of drinking and driving. Under no circumstances should he get into a car being driven by a friend who has been drinking. Explain about establishing a designated driver if drinking is to occur.

8. Teach your child to say no. Project D.A.R.E., a drug prevention program developed by the Los Angeles Police Department and the Los Angeles Unified School District, suggests eight ways to say no to drugs. Rehearse these with your child:

- Say, "No thanks."
- Give an excuse or a reason.
- Use the "broken record" technique—repeat the reason without giving in.
- Walk away.
- Change the subject.
- Avoid the situation.
- Give the cold shoulder to the person offering the drugs or alcohol.
- Find friends who don't use drugs or alcohol. There's strength in numbers.

Two More Things You Can Do

Project D.A.R.E. has been highly successful in Los Angeles. To date, it has expanded to 3,500 communities in all 50 states and has been adopted by several other countries, including Australia and Canada.

Project D.A.R.E. involves both the local police force and school district. A highly trained police officer visits kindergarten through fourth-grade classrooms to acquaint the children with the program. For fifth- and sixth-graders, the officer comes to class weekly to present lessons on the harmful effects of drugs, offering ways to resist drugs, interpret messages in the media, manage stress without drugs, build self-esteem, form a support system, and take a stand. The program continues with follow-up lessons in junior high and high school.

Project D.A.R.E. has met with great success, not only in reducing drug use, but also in lowering gang membership and violence. If such a program does not exist in your child's school, consider joining with other members of your community to implement one. (See the Resource Guide for whom to contact.) Finally, if your child is abusing alcohol or drugs, it is advisable to take him to counseling. Psychological guidance, coupled with a 12-step program such as Alateen (check the *White Pages* for a local Alcoholics Anonymous listing), can help children overcome their addiction.

Watch for Use of Marijuana and Other Drugs

C hildren begin smoking marijuana for the same reasons that they begin consuming alcohol: They may believe they have to do it to belong to the "in" crowd; they use drugs as a form of rebellion; or they may be numbing themselves to pain. A number of other reasons (see 44, Prevent Alcohol Abuse) might also prompt its use.

Most youngsters try marijuana in junior high according to the American Lung Association. But some even sample it in elementary school—as early as fourth or fifth grade! In fact, marijuana-related toys and paraphernalia, such as space guns and Frisbees, have been developed to appeal to just this age group.

The marijuana grown today can be as much as 10 times stronger than that of the sixties and seventies, and so its harmful effects are more pronounced. Moreover, unlike alcohol, which the body excretes within several hours after ingestion, the chemicals in marijuana can remain in the body for more than a month. And those chemicals are dangerous: Marijuana contains more cancer-causing substances than tobacco. It is also a lung irritant that can contribute to chronic bronchitis and emphysema.

In addition, the drug suppresses male and female hormone levels and interferes with normal sexual development and fertility. Marijuana use during puberty can have lifelong effects. In young women, for instance, it can interrupt normal ovulation and menstruation and in young men it can lower testosterone levels, thereby inhibiting fertility.

Marijuana is not physically addictive like alcohol, nicotine, cocaine, and heroin. But it is *psychologically* addictive, which means marijuana use can still seriously affect your youngster's future. The drug creates a sense of apathy and a loss of motivation. Children who regularly smoke marijuana lose interest in schoolwork. They may also use the drug to escape from making hard decisions and taking responsibility for their actions.

How Can You Tell If Your Child Is Using Marijuana?

Many of the signs of alcohol consumption also apply to smoking marijuana. Other signs include:

- ◆ Tiredness, apathy, lack of enthusiasm for favorite hobbies or schoolwork
- ◆ An unexplained decline in grades
- ◆ Red eyes and increased use of eyedrops
- ◆ Increased appetite
- ◆ Chronic cough or chest pains
- ◆ New friends coupled with loss of interest in old friends
- ◆ Untidiness
- ◆ Need for large sums of money or the disappearance of money or valuables from the home
- ◆ "Stash" boxes (unfamiliar locked containers), rolled and twisted cigarettes, plastic bags filled with an oregano-like substance, seeds, or plants.
- ◆ Drug-related comics, T-shirts, or books
- ◆ Drug paraphernalia: bongs, water pipes, roach clips, rolling papers, and the like)
- ◆ The smell of burning marijuana (like burnt rope)
- ◆ Incense, scented candles, or room deodorizers

If you find spoons, razor blades, straws, or mirrors, be advised that these may be used for cocaine.

Can You Prevent Habitual Marijuana Use?

University of California, Berkeley, psychologists Jonathan Shedler and Jack Block say it best in their study published in the May 1990 issue of *The American Psychologist:* Problem drug use among adolescents is "a symptom, not a cause, of personal and social maladjustment." Most adolescents will try marijuana. Indeed, according to this study, the best adjusted children experiment with the drug in a limited manner.

But those teenagers in the study who had become frequent users demonstrated personality traits by age 11 that differed from their better-adjusted peers. In the sixth grade, these future drug users were more often emotionally unstable, inattentive, uncooperative, stubborn, lacking in impulse control, rebellious, likely to become immobilized or withdrawn under stress, suspicious, and overreactive. Even as seven-year-olds, the youngsters who later became frequent drug users didn't get along well with their peers, were untrustworthy, had little concern for right and wrong, had difficulty establishing close relationships, and lacked confidence.

Interestingly, the parents of these children were perceived as being cold, hostile, critical, rejecting, underprotective, and unresponsive. They gave their children little encouragement yet pressured them to perform well. These parents seemed to lack pride in their kids and rarely praised them.

Clearly, educating your youngster to say no to drugs (see 44, Prevent Alcohol Abuse) is but one step in the drug-prevention process. Perhaps more meaningful, however, is the development of a close, warm relationship in which you support your youngster as he grows and develops. Permissiveness is not the key here. Rather, children are more likely to stay away from drugs when they receive lots of attention, affection, praise, and love from their parents and have reasonable expectations and limits placed on them. You will find several books in the Resource Guide that can help you establish just such a relationship.

If you find your child has become a frequent drug user, *family* counseling paired with a 12-step program is highly advisable.

PART
VI

Fire

Awareness

Eliminate Fire Hazards

People tend to underestimate how prevalent fire danger is in this country. According to the National Safety Council, a fire starts in an American home every 44 seconds, injuring 225,000 people and killing some 4,500 people annually.

Take action to protect your family before tragedy strikes. There is much you can do. Your first step is to check your home for fire hazards. Use the following checklist:

- Throw away stacks of old magazines, newspapers, or clothing that you may be storing in the garage or attic. These items are highly flammable and can feed a fire.
- Clear away grass, leaves, and brush from your home.
- Store ashes from your fireplace or barbecue in a metal trash can with a tight-fitting lid.
- Store oily rags in a metal trash can with a tight-fitting lid.
- Take extra care with cigarettes:
  - No smoking in bed or when drowsy (especially when under the influence of alcohol).
  - Don't abandon a lit cigarette in an ashtray. After burning down, the lit end can fall out of the tray onto a surface where it might cause a fire.
  - Never put ashes or extinguish cigarettes in wastepaper baskets.
  - Never light a cigarette near flammable liquids.
- Extinguish all candles before going to sleep or leaving the house.
- Pay attention to your electrical wiring:
  - Replace worn, frayed, or cracked wires with new UL-

approved wiring.
- ◆ Never nail wires down or run them over metal objects.
- ◆ Never run cords under rugs where, unbeknownst to you, they can become frayed.
- ◆ Avoid using "octopus" electrical outlets. Plugging too many appliances (especially heaters, irons, or toaster-ovens) into one outlet can overheat the circuit.

◆ Be sure to use proper fuses in your fuse box. If you're blowing fuses frequently, have your house wiring checked by a qualified electrician.

◆ Always disconnect your iron before leaving it, and be sure it's upright.

◆ Keep flammable objects, including draperies, away from heaters and light bulbs.

◆ If you're using a portable electric heater, be sure it has been UL approved.

◆ If you have a gas fireplace or need to light the pilot on your gas oven, always light the match before turning on the gas.

◆ Never use a lit match to detect a natural-gas leak. Call your gas company if you smell gas. Ventilate your home well. If the odor is very strong or you hear the hiss of escaping gas, evacuate your home and immediately notify the gas company.

◆ Keep a screen in front of your fireplace. Be sure it covers the entire surface.

◆ Install a spark arrester on your chimney. Have the soot cleaned out of your chimney and flue yearly to ensure they function properly and safely.

◆ Use approved dry-cleaning solvents and only outdoors; allow surfaces you've cleaned to dry outside as well. Use small amounts at a time. If you use these products in the garage, be sure the area is well ventilated and that you are far from any source of flame, such as the pilot light to your oven, furnace, water heater, or gas dryer.

◆ Store flammable liquids in small quantities in safety metal containers with tight lids that have been approved by Underwriters Laboratories or Factory Mutual (FM). Glass is too breakable.

◆ Never store or use flammable liquids near an open flame.

◆ Fireworks are illegal in many cities and states. Even if you can buy them legally, they are dangerous. Keep them out of your home.

◆ Have your furnace inspected yearly by a professional technician. Change or clean the filter yearly.

Matches and Your Children

Unfortunately, under some circumstances, children can also be a "fire hazard." Be sure that you keep all matches and cigarette lighters out of sight and out of reach of your youngster. Store your matches in metal containers that are difficult for your youngster to open, and teach your child the dangers of playing with fire.

By 9 or 10, your youngster will be old enough to learn how to light matches. Be sure she does this only under your supervision. Show her that she must close the matchbook cover and that she should strike the match away from both her and others. Occasionally, sparks or bits of lit match break off when a match is struck. Demonstrate that you extinguish any sparks that can ignite. In addition, have your child run cold water over any recently lit match before throwing it into the trash.

Equip Your Home with Smoke Detectors and Fire Extinguishers

Most residential fire fatalities occur while families are asleep—between the hours of 10 PM and 6 AM—according to the National Safety Council. Often, smoke and poisonous gases such as carbon monoxide released as a result of a smoldering fire cause death long before the flames do.

Smoke detectors awaken family members in time to escape before smoke or toxic fumes disorient (or kill) them. The National Fire Protection Association maintains that smoke detectors cut the risk of dying from a house fire by 50 percent.

Smoke Detectors

There are two types of smoke alarms: ionization and photoelectric. Ionization detectors react quickly to fires that give off little smoke and lots of flame, whereas the photoelectric variety is more sensitive to smoldering, smoky fires. Both are reliable warning systems. Just be sure whichever one you purchase has the UL or FM stamp of approval.

How Many Detectors Do You Need?

That depends on the size of your home, its layout, and the number of bedrooms. At the very least, you should install a detector in the hallway leading to the bedrooms. (If your home has a bedroom such as a maid's room or study off the kitchen area, be sure to place a detector in there as well.) If you live in a multistory dwelling, put detectors on each floor, including the basement.

Where Should You Place the Detectors?

Put the detectors either directly on the ceiling, about 12 inches away from any walls, or on the wall, 6 to 12 inches from the ceiling. Avoid installing detectors in corners, near air vents or windows, or in a bathroom. Consult the instructions in the package for further rules on how and where to install the detector.

How Should You Test the Detector?

Unfortunately, a smoke detector does little good if it's not in proper working order. Don't simply trust that yours works. Some experts estimate that as much as a third of the detectors installed in the U.S. are not functioning.

Certain smoke detectors beep loudly when the battery runs low. Others show a flashing light, and still others require you to push a test button or light a match near the grill. If your smoke detector has no automatic indicator, you should test it monthly, following the instructions in the package. Be sure to change batteries at least once a year. (You can use Christmas or New Year's as a reminder that it's time for a fresh start.)

Experts recommend that you frequently vacuum the detector grill to remove dust that might inhibit smoke detection.

Fire Extinguishers

Most home fires fall into three categories:

A — Those caused by common, easily combustible items in the home: paper, wood, cloth, plastic.

B — Those caused by flammable or combustible liquids such as gasoline, cleaning fluid, benzene, turpentine, alcohol, acetone, cooking oil, and charcoal lighter fluid. The accumulated fumes from flammable liquids (like gasoline, cleaning fluid, or acetone) can ignite at room temperature. Combustible liquids (like cooking oil or lighter fluid) must be heated before they create a fire hazard.

C — Those caused by electrical malfunction. Here there is a danger of electrical shock and fire. Never use water on such a fire because it conducts electricity.

The best fire extinguishers to buy are rated ABC—that is, they are able to douse fires of all three types. As with smoke detectors, be sure to buy extinguishers that are UL or FM approved.

Where to Place Fire Extinguishers

Keep your extinguishers accessible—not in a closet, where it can be buried under a pile of junk and difficult to find in an emergency! It's wise to have one extinguisher in the kitchen and another in the garage, as well as one on each level of your home. The National Safety Council suggests that extinguishers should be mounted near room exits that provide an escape route.

How to Use a Fire Extinguisher

Be sure to read and understand the product instructions. First, determine if you can safely fight the fire yourself. A 2$1/2$-pound extinguisher discharges its contents in 8 to 10 seconds. A 5-pound extinguisher lasts for 10 to 12 seconds. If the fire is too big for you to handle safely, evacuate the area. If you feel you can fight it, have someone call the fire department anyway. Firefighters will make sure that the fire has been completely quelled.

In general, to use the extinguisher, you should:

◆ Break the seal and remove the pin.
◆ Keep back—8 to 10 feet—from the fire, especially if it involves a flammable liquid. Otherwise, the fire retardants may splash the fire into other areas of the house.
◆ Aim the nozzle at the base of the fire, not at the smoke, and press the lever.
◆ Spray with a sweeping motion, moving from side to side. Keep the retardants flowing in a steady stream.

Extinguisher Maintenance

Inspect your fire extinguishers monthly. Be sure they are full and that the contents are under adequate pressure. (A round gauge at the top indicates pressure.) Recharge the extinguisher after each use, no matter how small. Fire-extinguisher companies provide this service.

Be Prepared: Know What to Do in Case of Fire

It's imperative that you and your family develop a plan in case of fire. You should hold fire drills once every six months, just to be sure that you all know what to do. It's even wise to hold surprise drills like administrators do at school. The Los Angeles Fire Department suggests that the following components be included in your safety plan:

♦ Despite your smoke detectors, it's a good idea to keep a whistle and a flashlight near your beds. The fire may block the hall connecting your bedrooms, so determine other ways you can alert your children (like blowing the whistle or pounding on the walls).

♦ Keep bedroom and hall doors shut when you sleep. Closed doors slow a fire's advance, prevent drafts that can fan flames, and can give you time to escape.

♦ All rooms in your home should have two exits—at least one door and one window. Make sure that family members know where the exits are.

♦ If you live in a two-story home, be sure you have a fire escape or a portable fire ladder. The latter is made of nonflammable rope and is hooked over a window sill to allow for exit.

♦ Choose a meeting place outside the home. This is crucial. If some family members are wandering about away from the designated spot, parents or firefighters may believe that they are still inside the burning structure.

♦ Teach your child never to hide under a bed or in a closet during a fire. If she detects smoke, she should blow her whistle and yell.

♦ Saving lives is more important than saving property. In case of fire, be sure your child knows to escape to the designated spot without searching for toys, shoes, or other belongings and without getting dressed.

◆ Explain to your child that once out of the house, she cannot return, not even to retrieve a favorite pet or doll. Once out, she must stay out.

What to Do in Case of Fire

Teach and practice these emergency measures with your family. Make them part of your fire drill.

◆ If you smell smoke or your smoke detector sounds the alarm, don't stand up. Rather, roll out of bed and *crawl* to the door: The air closest to the ground is safest, so stay low, under the smoke.

◆ Yell "Fire," blow your whistle, bang on the walls. Get your family's attention.

◆ Touch your bedroom door. If it feels hot at the top or if the hinges and knob are hot, don't open it. Doing so would create a draft that would draw the fire into your room.

◆ If the door is cool, open it a crack but be ready to close it quickly, if need be. Face away from the opening and once again alert other family members. Escape through the door if there is no smoke. Check all doors before you open them and close them as you exit, to help hamper the fire.

◆ Go to your predetermined meeting place. Do not return to the house.

◆ Call the fire department, dial 9-1-1, or dial 0 for the operator. Don't be the first to hang up.

◆ If the fire is in the hallway, your door will feel hot. Block the bottom of the door with rags or towels. Crawl to the window. Wrap yourself in your blanket and hang your head out for fresh air.

◆ Wave a blanket or sheet and yell for help.

◆ If you can climb out safely, do so. If not, wait for the fire department.

◆ If you live in an apartment, familiarize your children with staircases and fire escapes. Don't use the elevator in case of fire.

◆ If it's safe, call the fire department immediately, or after evacuating the house, go to a neighbor's home and call from there. Then go to your family's meeting place.

◆ In case her clothing catches fire, teach your child to *stop, drop,* and *roll.* Running will only fan the flames, while dropping and rolling will smother them. When rolling, your child should cover her face with her hands. (Purchase flame-resistant pajamas that meet federal regulations.)

It's also a good idea to visit your local fire station with your child. Many fire stations hold an open house once a year, and your youngster will be fascinated by the equipment while learning valuable safety lessons. If you're unwilling to wait for the open house, you can call the station and ask to make an appointment for a visit. Familiarity with firefighting equipment can allay some of your youngster's fears during an emergency.

Prevent Kitchen Fires

Experts estimate that a third of all home fires begin in the kitchen. Yet many are preventable. Learning appropriate safety measures can make all the difference. This is especially true if you must leave your youngsters home alone. (See 6, Teach Your Child Latchkey Safety for more information.)

Safety Measures You Can Take

♦ Keep combustible items away from the stove's heat and flames. Combustibles include kitchen and paper towels, and plastic bottles, particularly those containing cooking oil.

♦ Don't hang anything—spice or utensil racks, curtains, pots and pans—over the stove. Aside from the danger of flammable objects catching fire, you or your child may have to reach for items over boiling pots and flames.

♦ Turn pot handles parallel to or away from the front of the stove.

♦ Don't use towels or aprons to pick up hot pots. These can drag into the flames and catch fire. Keep oven mitts handy, but don't hang them above or leave them close to the stove.

♦ Clean oven hoods, vents, ovens, and broilers to prevent grease from accumulating.

♦ Never leave cooking food unattended. Most fires in the kitchen start with cooking food that has been ignored.

♦ Always check inside the oven before turning it on. You may have forgotten that you had stored a pot in there.

What to Do If a Grease Fire Starts in the Kitchen

First, a few pointers on what *not* to do:

- Don't simply turn the heat off and leave it at that. The pan may be hot enough so that the grease will continue burning.
- Don't throw water on a grease fire. It will only cause the fat to splatter up so that it may splash burning liquid around the kitchen.
- Don't throw flour on the fire to smother it. Flour is highly flammable—even explosive. (Some experts recommend baking soda as a smothering agent, but it needs to be lump-free and thrown in at the correct angle.)
- Don't attempt to move the burning pan. You'll create a draft that will feed the fire, and you'll also run the danger of splattering yourself.
- Don't turn on the vent or fan. That will feed the flames with more oxygen. In the worst case, the fan can suck flames up into the vent, spreading the fire to other parts of your house.

Here are things you *should* do in case of a grease fire:

- Use the pot lid to smother the flames. But don't try to drop the lid directly on the fire; you're apt to burn yourself. Instead:
  - With an oven mitt on, come at the fire from an angle.
  - Protecting yourself from smoke and flames, carefully lower the lid onto the pot. Totally covering the pot will smother the fire.
  - If the lid isn't handy or available, use a cookie sheet, a cutting board, or a larger pot—anything that you can place over the fire.
  - If a fire starts in the broiler, don't throw in water. Simply shut off the heat and keep the door closed. Eventually, the flames will exhaust themselves by using all the available oxygen.

Do a Fire-Safety Roundup

Install Proper Security Bars

The newspapers are replete with tragic stories of families who have burned to death in their homes, unable to open security bars that they had installed to prevent burglaries. If you are inclined to add security bars to your home, be sure they are the kind that can be sprung open from the inside. Fixed, immobile bars will imprison you and your family should fire strike.

Also, be sure that your screens are easily removable from inside your home and that windows can be opened with no trouble. The seconds saved in a fast escape can save lives.

Holiday Precautions

House fires have ruined many a Christmas. To be sure that your holiday doesn't go up in smoke, take the following safety measures:

- Keep the trunk of your Christmas tree in a pail of water, a water-filled tree stand, or wet sand.
- Set it up away from heaters and the fireplace.
- Check the decorative lights you will be placing on your tree and around the interior and exterior of your home. Be sure their wiring is in top condition.
- Use only nonflammable decorations.
- Never run electric cords around metal Christmas trees.
- Keep candles away from flammable materials, including your tree.
- Extinguish candles before going out or going to sleep.
- Candles should be displayed on safe, stable candlesticks.

◆ Keep gift wrappings away from the fireplace and heater.

Halloween also presents some fire risks. Make sure your child takes the following precautions:

◆ To light up the inside of your Jack-o-lantern, use a small flashlight instead of a candle.

◆ Be sure that all costumes and masks are fire resistant.

◆ Be sure that decorations are fire resistant and that they're hung away from the heater, fireplace, and other sources of heat.

◆ No matter the eerie effect, don't allow your child to hang cloth or paper directly on a light bulb.

Resource
Guide

Resource Guide

Y ou may find the following resources helpful in keeping your child safe. Each suggestion is preceded by the section number in the book, for easy reference.

1. For general information on poison:

> National Safety Council
> 444 North Michigan Avenue
> Chicago, IL 60611
> (800) 621-7619, Ext. 6900

2. *For general childproofing and safety products catalogues:*

> Perfectly Safe catalogues
> (800) 837-KIDS
>
> The Safety Zone catalogue
> 2515 East 43rd Street
> Chattanooga, TN 37422-7247
> (800) 999-3030

2. *For more information on childproofing:*

> The National Safe Kids Campaign
> 111 Michigan Avenue, NW
> Washington, DC 20010-2970
> (202) 939-4993
>
> National Safety Council
> 444 North Michigan Avenue
> Chicago, IL 60611
> (800) 621-7619, Ext. 6900

3. *For more information on radon gas:*

> The Environmental Protection Agency Radon Hotline:
> (800) SOS-RADON
>
> *You can also obtain information on radon from the EPA's* A Citizen's Guide to Radon, *and by contacting your local American Lung Association and Department of Health. Your state's Radon Office will provide you with a list of all radon-measurement companies that meet with state or EPA approval as well as other valuable information.*

4. For additional information about lead in dishes:

> California Department of Health Services
> Food and Drug Branch
> 714 P Street
> Sacramento, CA 95814
>
> Center for Food Safety and Applied Nutrition
> U.S. Food and Drug Administration
> 200 C Street, SW
> Washington, DC 20201

4. To find out about lead levels in your dishes, contact:

> Crownford China Co., (800) 892-4500
> Fitz & Floyd, (214) 918-0098
> Johnson Brothers, (800) 955-1550
> Lenox, (800) 635-3669
> Mikasa, (800) 833-4631
> Nikko, (201) 633-5100
> Noritake, (213) 537-9601
> Pfaltzgraff, (800) 999-2811
> Pickard, (708) 395-3800
> Portmeirion, (212) 889-3535
> Royal Doulton, (800) 682-4462
> Royal Worcester, (212) 683-7130
> Sasaki, (212) 686-5080
> Spode Limited, (212) 683-7130
> Syracuse, (800) 342-4111
> Villeroy & Boch, (800) 223-1762
> Wedgwood (800) 955-1550

4. For information on lead dust and lead in paint, along with names of lead-testing laboratories, "de-leading" contractors, and home lead test kits sanctioned by Consumers Union:

> The Lead Institute
> P.O. Box 591244
> San Francisco, CA 94118

5. For more information on babysitters:

> National Safety Council
> 444 North Michigan Avenue
> Chicago, IL 60611
> (800) 621-7619, Ext. 6900

5. For free information on choosing and screening an appropriate care-giver or day-care facility, send a self-addressed, stamped envelope (2 stamps) to:

> Child Care Action Campaign
> 330 7th Avenue, 17th floor
> New York, NY 10001
> (212) 239-0138

5. For a sample job questionnaire for potential babysitter candidates:

> "Childcare Form"
> *Child* Magazine
> 110 Fifth Avenue
> New York, NY 10011

6. *For more information on latchkey kids:*

> *The Parent/Child Manual on Latchkey Kids,*
> by Charlene Solomon (TOR Books: New York, 1989)

8. *For more information on toys and play equipment:*

> National Safety Council
> 444 North Michigan Avenue
> Chicago, IL 60611
> (800) 621-7619, Ext. 6900

9. *For more information on electrical wiring and appliances:*

> National Safety Council
> 444 North Michigan Avenue
> Chicago, IL 60611
> (800) 621-7619, Ext. 6900

11. *For more information on water safety and other environmental concerns such as lead and radon gas in the home:*

> *Home Safe Home: How to Make Your Home Environmentally Safe,* by William J. Kelly (National Press Books: Bethesda,1989)

11. *For information on water analysis labs and contaminants you should test for in your area:*

> Environmental Protection Agency Drinking Water
> Hotline
> (800) 426-4791

16. *For more information on asbestos in the home, contact your local American Lung Association to request these and other publications:*

> *Asbestos in Your Home*
> *Indoor Air Pollution Fact Sheet—Asbestos*
> *Air Pollution in Your Home?*

16. *For information on EPA-approved laboratories that analyze materials for asbestos content:*

> Laboratory Accreditation Administration
> The National Institute for Standards and Technology
> Gaithersburg, MD 20899
> (301) 975-4016

16. *For qualified roofers who perform asbestos-correction work:*

> (800) USA-ROOF
> In Illinois, call: (708) 318-6722

16. *For information on asbestos in floors, send a stamped, self-addressed business-size envelope to:*

> Resilient Floor Covering Institute
> 966 Hungerford Drive, Suite 12-B
> Rockville, MD 20850
> Request "Recommended Work Procedures
> for Resilient Floor Covers"

16. For information on asbestos in consumer products (such as certain hair dryers):

> Consumer Product Safety Commission
> Washington, DC 20207
> Hotline: (800) 638-CPSC

16. For identification of asbestos in your home, contact the Asbestos Coordinator in your state's Environmental Protection Agency Regional Office. For information on the Environmental Protection Agency's asbestos programs and to find out if your state trains and certifies asbestos removal contractors:

> Environmental Protection Agency
> (202) 554-1404

17. For more information on gunproofing your child:

> *Gun-Proof Your Children,* by Massad Ayoob (1986)
> Police Bookshelf
> 70 Broadway
> Concord, NH 03301
> (603) 224-6814
> $4.95 plus $2 for shipping
>
> *Brian's Message* (video)
> Brian's Message, Inc.
> P.O. Box 650886
> Vero Beach, FL 32665
> $15

18. For more information on traffic safety:

> National Safety Council
> 444 North Michigan Avenue
> Chicago, IL 60611
> (800) 621-7619, Ext. 6900

> The National Safe Kids Campaign
> 111 Michigan Avenue, NW
> Washington, DC 20010-2970
> (202) 939-4493

18. For more information on bicycle safety:

> National Safety Council
> 444 North Michigan Avenue
> Chicago, IL 60611
> (800) 621-7619, Ext. 6900

> The National Safe Kids Campaign
> 111 Michigan Avenue, NW
> Washington, DC 20010-2970
> (202) 939-4493

22–29. For more information about resources on child sexual abuse and exploitation, and abuse in the child-care setting, contact:

> The National Center for Missing and Exploited Children
> Publications Department
> 2101 Wilson Boulevard, Suite 550
> Arlington, VA 22201-3052
> (703) 235-3900

24-hour hotline for those with information on missing or exploited children: (800) 843-5678

National Committee for the Prevention of Child Abuse
332 South Michigan Avenue, Suite 1600
Chicago, IL 60604
(312) 663-3520

Child Help U.S.A.
24-hour national hotline
(800) 422-4453

Child Care Action Campaign
330 Seventh Avenue, 17th floor
New York, NY 10001
(212) 239-0138

31. For more information on disaster preparedness, contact your local American Red Cross chapter and ask for:

The Family Survival Guide
Brochure number: 329195

32. For more information on choosing the right afterschool program for your child:

The Parent/Child Manual on Daycare,
by Charlene Solomon (TOR Books: New York, 1989)

35. For more information on AIDS:

> The National AIDS Hotline
> (800) 342-AIDS

> The U.S. Department of Health and Human Services
> Public Health Services
> Centers for Disease Control
> (404) 639-3311

> National AIDS Information Clearinghouse
> P. O. Box 6003
> Rockville, MD 20850
> (800) 458-5231

36. For more information on first aid:

> National Safety Council
> 444 North Michigan Avenue
> Chicago, IL 60611
> (800) 621-7619, Ext. 6900

36. For First Aid Pocket Guide:

> American Red Cross
> Oregon Trail Chapter
> P.O. Box 3200
> Portland, OR 97208
> (503) 284-1234

37. For workbooks on CPR and rescue breathing for children, contact your local chapter of the American Red Cross.

40. For a free copy of the Food Guide Pyramid write to:

> U.S. Department of Agriculture
> Washington, DC 20250

40. For a free guide to foods high in fiber, call:

> American Cancer Society
> (800) ACS-2345

40. For more information on proper nutrition contact:

> American Heart Association
> National Center
> 7320 Greenville Avenue
> Dallas, TX 75231
> Ask for the brochure, *Diet in the Healthy Child*
>
> Center for Science in the Public Interest
> 1875 Connecticut Avenue
> Washington, DC 20009
>
> Food and Drug Administration
> Consumer Inquiries
> 5600 Fishers Lane
> Rockville, MD 20857

41. For more information on sun exposure and skin cancer:

> Skin Cancer Foundation
> Box 561, Department AB
> New York, NY 10156

41. For a free 0.3-ounce sample of DuraScreen PABA-free sunscreen, call:

> Penederm Inc.
> (800) 395-DERM

42. For more information on contaminated fish, refer to:

> "Is Our Fish Fit to Eat?"
> *Consumer Reports*, Volume 57, February 1992, p. 103

> "Mercurial Risks from Acid's Reign: Tainted Fish May Pose a Serious Human Health Hazard," by Janet Raloff, *Science News*, Vol. 139, March 9, 1991, p. 152

42. For more information on mercury in dental fillings refer to:

> "When Your Patients Ask About Mercury in Amalgam," *Journal of the American Dental Association*, Vol. 120, April 1990, p. 395

> "Ethics and Dental Amalgam Removal," by John G. Odom, Ph.D.
> *Journal of the American Dental Association*, Vol. 122, June 1991, p. 69

43, 45. For antismoking and marijuana information, including coloring and activity books, contact:

> The American Lung Association
> 1740 Broadway
> New York, NY 10019-4374
> (212) 315-8700

43. For more information on smoking and cancer, contact:

> The American Cancer Society
> 1599 Clifton Road, NE
> Atlanta, GA 30329
> (800) ACS-2345

44. For more information on alcoholism:

> Alcoholics Anonymous
> 475 Riverside Drive
> New York, NY 10115
> (212) 870-3400

44. For more information on drinking and driving:

> Mothers Against Drunk Driving (MADD)
> 511 E. John Carpenter Freeway, Suite 700
> Irving, TX 75062-8187
> (214) 744-6233

> Students Against Drunk Driving (SADD)
> P.O. Box 800
> Marlboro, MA 01752
> (508) 481-3568

44–45. *For more information on drug-abuse prevention:*

Drug Abuse Resistance Education
(DARE)
P.O. Box 2090
Los Angeles, CA 90051
(800) 223-DARE

Parents' Resource Institute for Drug Education (PRIDE)
The Hurt Bldg.
50 Hurt Plaza
Atlanta, GA 30303
(404) 577-4500

National Clearinghouse for Alcohol and Drug Information
P.O. Box 2345
Rockville, MD 20852
(301) 468-2600
(Provides a publication list on request)

National Council on Alcoholism and Drug Dependence
12 West 21st Street
New York, NY 10010
(800) NCA-CALL

Families Anonymous
P.O. Box 528
Van Nuys, CA 91408
(818) 989-7841

Center for Substance
Abuse Prevention's
Workplace Helpline
(800) 843-4971

The American Council for Drug Education (ACDE)
6193 Executive Boulevard
Rockville, MD 20852
(301) 294-0600

44–45. For a list of drug- or alcohol-related parent support groups:

National Federation of Parents for Drug-Free Youth
P.O. Box 722
Silver Spring, MD 20901
(301) 649-7100

45. For more information on the psychological components of marijuana, refer to:

"Adolescent Drug Use and Psychological Health: A
Longitudinal Study," by Jonathan Shedler and Jack
Block, *American Psychologist,* May 1990,
Vol. 45, pp. 612

45. For more information on creating a loving relationship with your child while keeping him or her within your limits, see:

Disciplining Your Preschooler and Feeling Good About It, by
Mitch Golant, Ph.D., and Susan K. Golant (Lowell
House: Los Angeles,1987)

Getting Through to Your Kids, by Susan K. Golant, M.A.,
and Mitch Golant, Ph.D. (Lowell House: Los Angeles,
1991)

Finding Time for Fathering by Mitch Golant, Ph.D., and Susan K. Golant, M.A. (Ballantine Books: New York, 1992)

46–50. For more information on fire safety, contact your local fire department as well as:

National Safety Council
444 North Michigan Avenue
Chicago, IL 60611
(800) 621-7619, Ext. 6900

Ask for the following brochures and bulletins:
Safety Bulletin No. 2: Home Fire Safety
Fire Safety at Home
Surviving Hotel Fires
Your Home Safety Checklist

47. For more information on smoke detectors:

"Smoke Detectors—A Fire Safety Basic"
National Fire Protection Association
Public Affairs Office
Dept. TFH
P.O. Box 9101
1 Batterymarch Park
Quincy, MA 02269
(617) 770-3000